TRADING UP

UP

MOVING
FROM
SUCCESS

TO SIGNIFICANCE
ON WALL STREET

D0711332

David—

Blessings on your journey!

Eph. 2:10

Darry.

48.5.10

"An early mentor of mine convinced me early in my walk with Christ that you can never argue with a person's testimony. It's true and unique to them and reveals what they have experienced in life. This book, *Trading Up*, is a personal testimony of one of the most successful financial advisors in the country. He traces his life as moving from success to significance, and I have personally witnessed that over, probably, 12 to 15 years of relationship with Jeff. This book is a compelling story that will challenge you greatly in regards to your perspective, the real driver of all financial decision making. I am so delighted that Jeff put his story on paper and that it can be shared with, hopefully, millions of others. It is true, and it is compelling."

— RON BLUE, Founding Director, Kingdom Advisors

"In *Trading Up*, Jeff Thomas unravels the deceitfulness of worldly "success" and reveals the joy of abiding in Christ as a marketplace leader. Jeff's transparency, humility, and energy draw his audience into a personal reflection of the journey toward true significance."

— DR. CHRIS HOLDORF, CEO, National Christian Foundation

"A great read. Jeff's story illuminates a path that leads to success and significance at the same time."

— DEAN NIEWOLNY, Halftime

"We all have a story, but most people focus on the woes of their past and have a hard time reconciling the immediate and the eternal. Jeff Thomas has, again, broken away from the ordinary and proven himself extraordinary. In *Trading Up*, he gives us an inside look at his past with a focus on the wisdom gained through experience and relationships. Get ready for his authentic considerations of what distracts most and what matters most; you won't be able to put it down!"

— **BOB SHANK**, Founder/CEO, The Master's Program

"If more leaders can let Jeff's experiences save them from the "hollow golden egg" by pressing into the gnawing sense of "there must be more" to find their true destiny, the world would be a better place. Read it, and trade up for the best life!"

— **MIKE SHARROW**, CEO, The C12 Group

"My friend, Jeff Thomas, reminds us that God's wisdom about money will change your life! He knows because he has lived it!"

— **HOWARD DAYTON**, Founder, Compass

"Jeff's story illustrates a clear connection between Biblical principles and business practices. Leaders can trade up in business to a higher purpose."

— **CLIFF ROBINSON**, SVP/Chief People Officer,
   Chick-Fil-A

"Jeff's story illustrates, once again, that generosity is the antidote for greed. That is a truly great trade!"

—**TODD HARPER**, President, Generous Giving

TRADING UP

MOVING FROM SUCCESS

TO SIGNIFICANCE ON WALL STREET

JEFF THOMAS

HIGH BRIDGE BOOKS
HOUSTON

Trading Up
by Jeff Thomas

Copyright © 2019 by Jeff Thomas
All rights reserved.

Printed in the United States of America
ISBN (Paperback): 978-1-946615-44-2

All rights reserved. Except in the case of brief quotations embodied in critical articles and reviews, no portion of this book may be reproduced, stored in a retrieval system, or transmitted in any form or by any means—electronic, mechanical, photocopy, recording, scanning, or other—without the prior written permission from the author.

THE HOLY BIBLE, NEW INTERNATIONAL VERSION®, NIV® Copyright © 1973, 1978, 1984, 2011 by Biblica, Inc.® Used by permission. All rights reserved worldwide.

High Bridge Books titles may be purchased in bulk for educational, business, fundraising, or sales promotional use. For information, please contact High Bridge Books via
www.HighBridgeBooks.com/contact.

Published in Houston, Texas by High Bridge Books

Contents

For my wife, Dolly, who teaches me
about generosity every day

Prologue

*Why do I have three Super Bowl rings and still
think there's something greater out there for me? I
mean, maybe a lot of people would say, 'Hey man,
this is what is.' I reached my goal, my dream, my
life. I think, 'God, it's got to be more than this.' I
mean this isn't, this can't be what it's all cracked up
to be. I love playing football, and I love being the
quarterback for this team. But at the same time, I
think there are a lot of other parts about me that I'm
trying to find.*

—Tom Brady, New England Patriots' Quarterback

Have you ever had a great victory in life that left you asking, "Is
that all there is?" I have. That's what this book is about—
my journey of *trading up* from a focus on earthly success to
a focus on eternal significance. My story took place on Wall
Street, but the same trade is available to everyone on every
street, and I hope my story inspires you to make it.

In 1995, I was a rookie broker with exactly zero clients.
Within five short years, I became what everyone in the busi-
ness wanted to be—a one-million-dollar ($1mm) producer.
I eventually grew the business to over $2mm in production.
I should have been on top of the world, right? That's what

I thought. However, all I could think about was that if I died at that time, my epitaph would read, "Here lies Jeff. He made rich people richer." Not exactly the life purpose I was after.

Mine is also the unlikely story of how a pastor's kid (PK), who didn't even know that there was such a thing as a financial advisor growing up, ended up as one of the top advisors in the country. As it turned out, my background — a PK and a competitive tennis player — was the perfect foundation for my career. I knew what it meant to take care of a flock from watching my father, and I knew what it meant to be self-reliant from playing untold singles matches.

Fewer than one percent of advisors in 2000 produced $1mm in revenue. Even fewer got there in five years. At multiple Morgan Stanley meetings of top advisors, management declared that the steep statistics of failure for financial advisors haven't changed in over 70 years — 90% of new advisors fall out of the business within three years. However, in the middle of what seemed to be a great success story, things took an unexpected turn. Having achieved the financial success that I was striving after, I came to discover that the golden egg was hollow. That the happiness, joy, and satisfaction I assumed would be greeting me when I finally climbed to the top had left for vacation — permanent vacation.

It was then that I began looking to the roots of my childhood faith for answers. Striving for financial success was not a big topic of conversation around the dinner table growing up. Things like the joy and satisfaction of serving others, God's unerring wisdom in planning our lives, and the role of faith in everyday life were authentically modeled for me. The impact of those lessons lingered within me. It was a return to those lessons that held the key to re-igniting my passion for the business. As I began to grow again in my faith, I discovered a game-changing truth that had been eluding me in my frantic pursuit to get to the top. Success and significance are two completely different commodities. But so many people believe—as I once did—that if you gain success, significance inevitably follows.

How then does one find genuine and lasting significance? In a phrase, you must *trade up* from a focus on success to a focus on significance.

I am still a financial advisor today. I love what I do. But I love it for far different reasons than before. And that is what this book is about. My journey has been filled with passion, hard work, arrogance, emptiness, clarity, and finally, joy and contentment. My focus on significance has led to success of a different kind. My hope and purpose for writing this book is to invite you to join me in the great adventure of *Trading Up*.

My disillusionment came in ll·5.

1

Roots

If I have seen further than others, it is by standing upon the shoulders of giants.

—Isaac Newton

Alex Haley, the author of *Roots*, kept a unique picture in his office. It was the portrait of a turtle sitting on top of a fence post. When asked why he liked the picture, he always replied, "Anytime you see a turtle up on top of a fence post, you know he had some help."

I love his perspective! Nobody gains success unaided. We are all turtles atop our own fence posts, and we were lifted there on other people's shoulders. At least I know that I was. And the two earliest sets of shoulders for me were also the most influential. They were my mother and father.

My father's name was Lew, and my mother's name was Louise. They were both raised in the small oil town of Bradford, Pennsylvania. My father was the youngest of four boys. His father (my grandfather) worked in the oilfield and died when my father was eight years old. My grandmother was given a little time before she had to move out of the company-owned housing outside of town in Lewis

Run. She used that time to get her teaching certificate so that she could work to support her four hungry boys. Grandma Thomas modeled a strong work ethic as well as a strong faith.

She instilled that faith in all of her sons. As a teenager, my dad became the youngest elder their little rural church had ever elected. His three older brothers thought they found their best opportunity in the military, so they all enlisted right out of high school. Dad was fortunate enough to earn a scholarship from Dresser Industries, which enabled him to attend the University of Cincinnati on a work-study program. He earned a mechanical engineering degree at the University of Cincinnati and subsequently earned what was essentially an MBA for engineers at Purdue University.

My mother was two years younger than my father and lived "on the other side of the tracks" from my father in Bradford. I say "the other side of the tracks" because my mom's father (Grandpa Knapp) had an office job with Kendall Oil. Even though Grandpa Knapp did not have a college degree, he and Grandma Knapp were able to provide their four children with a very nice house in town, as well as the college education he never received. My mother's parents were also committed believers and were very active in their local Presbyterian church. All four of the Knapp children and all four of the Thomas children followed their parents' lead as committed believers.

Although they grew up just miles apart and attended the same high school in a town with a population of 17,000, they didn't know each other. They were set up on a blind date while they were in college and married after my mother graduated from Ball State with an elementary education degree. They then moved to Terre Haute, Indiana, where my father took his first job with International Harvester. He was helping design the first SUV—the Scout. And it was in Terre Haute that my father was confronted with a question that would dramatically change the trajectory of our family forever. It was a question that was more than a question; it was also an assumption—an assumption that I believe has been, and continues to be, nothing short of devastating to the church and the cause of Christ. An assumption that has taken me years to break free from.

"Have you ever thought about entering 'the ministry'?"

That was the question posed by my parents' pastor to my then businessman/father in his late 20s. Now, this pastor was a good man with nothing but the best intentions in asking my father that question. He was also unwittingly trapped in a system that much of the Christian world continues to be trapped in to this day. In asking this well-intentioned question, there was a tragic assumption behind it. The assumption behind it was this: you are not *presently* in the ministry. And to be "in the ministry," you need to leave the business world to go to a special school that will prepare you so that you can then go out and serve God "full time." Nobody will quite put it this way, but the very implicit message behind the question of entering "the ministry" is essentially this: if your paycheck comes from a for-profit business, you are not presently firing on all cylinders for God. If you are willing to sell fully out to Him, then it means leaving your worldly occupation so that you can devote yourself to "the ministry." In other words, you could not possibly be in "the ministry" if you're still working at your "secular" occupation at the same time. This paradigm is so widely held that hardly anyone seems to question it. I love Dorothy Sayers' great word on this:

> It is the business of the church to recognize that the secular vocation, as such, is sacred. Christian people, and particularly perhaps the Christian clergy, must get it firmly into their heads that when a man or woman is called to a particular job of secular work, that is as true a vocation as though he or she were called to specifically religious work.

Again, my parents' pastor had only the best intentions, but, make no mistake, his questions could have been translated as, "Do you want to be a full-time pastor of a church like me?"

"Yes," my father replied. That one simple, honest answer put my parents on a whole new path.

I figured that the only person more shocked to hear my dad's "yes" than the pastor was my mom. I often think about what she must have thought at that moment! Here she had married this businessman on the fast-track, and he just said "yes" to the church ministry! I picture her leaning in and saying, "I'm sorry, what did you say?" I think she could be forgiven if she wanted to lay down some fleeces or ask God to perform some other miracles to confirm what she just heard!

However, when I asked my mom about that decision, she always just told it matter-of-factly as though she wasn't very surprised. She did say that dad decided to take what she considered to be the two hardest classes first (Greek and Hebrew) as a test to see if he wanted to continue. I wonder if she wasn't secretly hoping he would fail at those! Well, he didn't, and off they went to Pittsburgh Theological Seminary.

After graduating from seminary (and working summers for International Harvester), my dad's first associate pastor role was in Marion, Indiana. My sister and I were born there. We lived there in the late 1960s for just a couple of years and then moved to Cadiz, Ohio, for his next church assignment. In 1976, Dad took a position at the First Presbyterian Church in Kirkwood, Missouri (a suburb of St. Louis). It was there that my mother pursued her master's degree in education, and my dad completed his doctorate at Eden Seminary. My father's doctoral thesis centered on how to run the local church more efficiently and effectively using the business principles he had learned in his earlier career.

Growing up as a PK was a wonderful and sometimes surreal experience. The expectations placed on pastors and their families can be too high. PKs have a reputation for being problem children—probably due to the common rebellion that comes from living under the weight of those expectations. My sister and I rebelled some (as normal teenagers), but my parents were not heavy-handed and managed to give us a pretty normal upbringing. Somehow, we escaped childhood with many more positive memories than scars.

One of my favorite activities during high school and college summers was playing golf with my dad and his buddies. I really enjoyed the guys my dad hung out with. They were high-capacity men who drew their paychecks from various sources. One of them was a chaplain at a hospital. Another was a middle school teacher. Others were businessmen. But the thing I remember most was my exposure to strong Christians who were *not* pastors. My dad told me on many occasions that he liked hanging out with those guys because they didn't expect him to be perfect as "The Pastor." That perspective has given me a heart for pastors and their families and an insight into one of their big challenges. My father's faith, and that of his friends, was not stiff, sanctimonious, or boring. They laughed, kidded around, enjoyed the great game of golf as a gift from God, and thoroughly enjoyed being in community on the links. This exposure had a far greater impact on me than I ever realized at the time.

Apparently, everyone around me expected me to be a pastor like my father—except me! I came in second in the voting for "Most Likely to Be a Pastor" by my high school class. The guy who actually came in first was only voted in because he was easily riled, and when teased, would respond by retorting, "You are going to hell!"

I figured out pretty early on that being a pastor came with the responsibilities of a CEO but on a janitor's salary! That didn't seem like a great deal to a kid who was mowing lawns and programming the family computer to keep track of his savings. However, the benefits of being a PK greatly outweighed the financial challenges. My sister and I were raised in the church around a lot of wonderful, generous, kind, God-loving people. I was so, so fortunate to be exposed to a winsome, authentic, vibrant brand of spirituality which gave me a wonderful foundation. But, no matter how wonderful the parishioners were, I didn't think they were anywhere near as committed as my dad was. To me, since they didn't work for a non-profit, I didn't consider them to be "in ministry."

One of the only other professions I considered to be "in ministry" was a missionary. When I was about 10 years old, my parents told me that we had been invited to some parishioners' home for dinner because they were hosting a family of missionaries from New Guinea. I had no interest in going because I knew no one involved. However, since I was about the same age as the missionaries' son, I was dragged to the dinner to provide entertainment for him. What I remember most about that whole evening was that this boy did not own a pair of shoes! Seriously. They bought him a pair to come to the U.S. He had feet built for the jungle with these incredible callouses on the bottom of his feet like I had never seen before and have never seen since.

A couple of years later, while in middle school, I remember working a booth in the Fellowship Hall of our Church during "Missions Sunday." My booth contained a display from Heifer's International—a great organization that lives on today, providing farm animals and supplies to families in the developing world to give them a hand up, not just a handout. I remember sitting at my little booth with a small, wicker basket on the table in front of me, ready to receive donations. I thought I might get a few five- and ten-dollar bills, and I did. However, I also got a big surprise that day. One of my classmates' father casually walked over to my table, got out his checkbook, wrote something on a check, and handed it to me with no great ceremony. When he walked away, I looked at the check. It was for $500! To me, that represented my pay on 50 mown lawns! That gift made a big impact on me. I was impressed that the giver didn't make any show of it at all, and I knew that my family was unlikely to be able to make that kind of gift. I thought to myself, *Only a business person can make that kind of a gift.* That guy didn't just buy a new tractor for a farmer that day. He also inspired a kid who loved business and God.

My upbringing was full of crosscurrents that it took me years to navigate. I had a fundamental belief that the only people "all in" for God were people who received their paychecks from a non-profit. After all, that was the example that was set for me by my father. He "felt the call" to ministry, and for him (and therefore for me), that meant chucking his business career and going to seminary to be a church pastor.

On the other hand, I was exposed to a lot of God-fearing business people who were living authentic lives for Christ.

And that raises a question that I have struggled with all my life—what does it mean to be "all in" for God? Does it mean roaming barefoot through the jungles of New Guinea? Does it mean leaving one's job with International Harvester to go to seminary and then the pastorate? Does it mean staying on Wall Street to make a difference for the kingdom? I think the specifics of the answer will vary from person to person. But as for me, I'll always be so thankful for two parents who gave me an amazing example of what it meant to be "all in" for them. During my early success as a financial advisor, I credited my hard work and dedication to my success, but as I look back, I realize I was a turtle on a fence post. God gave me the resources I needed to be successful. He gave me parents who provided a great example, health, education, and a rising stock market! My success had a lot less to do with me than with Him.

Trading Tip #1

Never forget who brought you to the dance. Gratitude and humility are two of the soul's mightiest pillars for sustaining a joyous and truly significant life.

Question to Ponder

How would you define or describe being "all in" for God?

2

Turning Up the Volume: My Roaring 20's

 I am not young enough to know everything.

— Oscar Wilde

My first job out of Trinity University was in Houston. Before moving there, I had only visited the city once before. That previous trip had been a road trip from San Antonio, during college, to watch the Astros play in the "8th Wonder of the World"—the Astrodome. From our nosebleed seats, I had two lasting impressions. First, the place was huge and amazing. I had never been in a domed stadium. Secondly, I remember how quiet and subdued it was compared to the raucous St. Louis Cardinals games I had so enjoyed as a kid. It was at that game that I came to realize that not everyone in every MLB town hangs on every pitch. In St. Louis, there are two topics everyone is comfortable with—the weather and the Cardinals. (I will say, that after the Houston Astros won the World Series in 2017, Houston has become much more of a baseball town.)

At that time, in 1990, right out of college, I had another offer from a Big 8 accounting firm in St. Louis, but I thought there would be more opportunity in the much-larger Houston where I could carve a reputation for myself, instead of riding my father's coattails in St. Louis. I also felt some loyalty to Arthur Andersen, where I ended up working, since they had given me a scholarship as one of the top three accounting majors at Trinity. All three recipients went to work there. At that time, the Houston office of Andersen was one of the three largest in the country, holding its own alongside Chicago and New York.

Arthur Andersen had agreed to pay me the princely sum of $26,000 per year (plus overtime). I was honored to be there. I started along with about 100 other "newbies" that summer of 1990.

I had a budget for how much I could spend on rent. Andersen assigned me the same apartment locator that every other new recruit had been given. She started near downtown and kept driving her shiny Cadillac west on the main drag, Westheimer Road, until she reached an apartment complex that I said I could afford. I ended up at the West Point apartments at Westheimer near Fondren. I soon found out that I was further out than almost any of my peers. I had student loans to pay off, so my budget was tight. The apartment was $425 per month, all bills paid. The place was full of hard-working, generous blue-collar folks. One of my neighbors was an ex-con, one was an auto mechanic who generously repaired my ancient car regularly, and another was a guy who must have had a dozen fish tanks. My fish-loving neighbor claimed he lived there because the electric bill for the tanks was more than his total rent!

At that time, there were three basic divisions of Andersen—Audit, Tax, and Consulting. The accounting majors got to choose between Audit and Tax. I chose Audit. I felt it would afford me the opportunity to get out of the office, meet more people, get to know the city, and learn more about other businesses.

Within Audit, there were two divisions—Energy and Commercial. In the Energy Division, you could spend nearly your entire year on one client. Since I was interested in learning about as many different businesses as possible, I chose the Commercial Division. In reality, the Commercial Division was a catch-all for "everything but energy."

Working for Andersen was a great experience. The training was first class. I had incredibly smart people surrounding me, and we worked hard, really hard. During busy season, it was not uncommon to work eight to 10 hours on one audit and then immediately drive to a second one for another four-plus hours. I don't know what I made per hour, but it was very likely less than my neighbor mechanic. It didn't matter because, for most of us, it was a training ground for different financial jobs down the line.

During my second year at Andersen, I was assigned to work in the "War Room" for the Resolution Trust Corporation (the "RTC" as it was commonly known) in Washington D.C. The RTC was a U.S. government-owned asset management entity charged with liquidating assets, primarily real estate-related assets, of savings and loan associations (S&Ls) declared insolvent as a consequence of the banking crisis of the 1980s.

I enjoyed my time in Washington D.C. Every morning, I would leave my corporate apartment and take the subway to the office in Columbus Circle. I was part of a team that was responsible for selling off the assets the government had taken off the balance sheets of all of those failed S&Ls.

There is one story from that experience that is burned into my memory. I remember a middle-aged man coming into the conference room where data was kept on all of the assets for sale. I don't remember his name, but let's call him Gordon. Gordon and his team spent hours reviewing the documents. After much study, his team decided to make an offer on a package of assets that had been valued at nearly $50mm just a few years before. Our team sold him those commercial properties for close to $10mm. I was the "keeper of the spreadsheet" for the sales and the tracking of assets in inventory, so I remember it well.

In the prior year of working at Andersen, I had spent time auditing plenty of successful companies. However, I had spent most of my time in some backroom adding up numbers. I was generally exposed to only my fellow Andersen teammates and the lower level financial reporting folks for the companies who would answer our detailed questions about the companies' financial statements.

This experience in the War Room for the RTC was different. This was my first real exposure to high-level dealmakers, and I liked being around them. I will never forget our team finalizing the sale of those properties to Gordon. I can still picture the scene in slow motion. I remember the magnificent suit Gordon was wearing. It was light tan and must have had some silk in it because it shimmered in a way my $100 poly-blend suit certainly did not! I didn't know how much it cost or who made it; all I knew was that it was way better than what I had and that I wanted to trade up for one like it!

The slow-motion scene continued as Gordon wheeled around after closing the deal and smiled one of the largest smiles that I can ever remember witnessing. It seemed to say, "I just made $10mm!" He walked out of the conference room through the glass doors, high-fived his partners, and disappeared down the hall. At that moment, I knew I was on the wrong side of that transaction! I entertained thoughts of quitting my job right there and going out to raise capital to buy depressed assets as this guy had done.

"Would that be a conflict of interest?" I asked myself. "Would it be possible to go from the keeper of the spreadsheet to the purchaser of the line items on that spreadsheet?" I went to sleep many nights that summer replaying that slow-motion vignette in my head. My eventual sad conclusion was that even if I discovered that it wasn't a conflict of interest to move to the other side of the table, I didn't have the contacts required to raise the capital as a 22-year-old, one year out of college. While I was unprepared to trade up to a new job like the one that tan-suit-wearing guy had at that moment, I promised myself that I would be ready the next time such an opportunity came along.

The truth be told, I wasn't a great auditor. While I really enjoyed my experience with Andersen, I craved more time with people and a view of the bigger picture. To put it mildly, the big picture is not something you see much of as a staff auditor. As is very common for people with a couple of years of experience in that business, I began interviewing for corporate positions.

I particularly remember one interview with a large, multinational company for an internal audit position. They asked me what I wanted out of my next job, and I told them I would like the ability to see a little more of the big picture.

I'll never forget the face of my interviewer when I said that. As soon as the sound waves hit her ears, I knew I wasn't getting the job. And I was right!

The next opportunity came a short time later. A recruiter called me and asked if I would be interested in interviewing for a job as an internal "senior" auditor with PaineWebber, one of the largest brokerage firms in the country. While I didn't love the idea of being an internal auditor, this was a little more interesting opportunity than I viewed most internal audit jobs to be. For one thing, it was in an industry that I enjoyed. I had audited quite a few financial institutions, including one brokerage firm, and found the business interesting. I thought this opportunity would be a good way to learn more about the industry. Secondly, the job had the added benefit of meeting a lot of people through traveling to various branches.

I started with PaineWebber in October of 1992. There was a small group of us based in Houston, which allowed for cheaper flights to the West Coast than did our New York headquarters. I thoroughly enjoyed the job. I spent nearly two-and-a-half years visiting close to 150 offices all over the western half of the United States and learned a ton about the wealth management business.

Like at Andersen, I really enjoyed the people I worked with. Generally, three of us would travel two weeks per month to the various branches, performing audits. The other two weeks were spent back in Houston, writing reports to management. I loved seeing the country. Our department was mostly made up of 20-somethings, so we had a built-in group of friends to see new cities with. The pay was a little better than at Andersen. I was now making a whopping $35k per year with the chance for a small bonus at the end of the year! I also got a one-time bonus for passing the CPA exam.

One of the perks of the job was the frequent-traveler points. My co-workers and I had maximizing points down to a science. Those points became part of my scorecard called "savings." Most of our points came from Continental Airlines and Marriott hotels. We thought of those points as a significant part of our pay. One year, my friend and co-worker, James, and I took it as a personal challenge to see how far we could go on 25k Continental miles. We were quite proud of ourselves for making it all the way to the Dominican Republic. As we rode a shuttle to our all-inclusive resort, I was struck by the plight of the Dominican people we passed. Most of them were working long, difficult hours in the fields. I realized that while I was busy playing a game of "how many points can I accumulate," these locals were concerned with far more basic needs. It reminded me of the kind of people my family's "all in" missionary friends served. I thought, *What am I supposed to do about these people? I am just a businessman, right? I am not in ministry.*

Being a saver by nature, during this time, I was able to stash away some cash. Beyond the benefits of seeing new cities and accruing points, the internal audit job also offered a small per-diem that allowed me to save some additional funds. In 1994, four years into my career, I had saved enough for a down payment on a modest home. I started looking at duplexes in the Museum District of Houston close to downtown. Houston real estate was still recovering from its downturn during the oil bust of the early- to mid-1980s and the banking crisis of the late '80s. I enlisted the help of a real estate agent in the neighborhood who patiently worked with this 25-year-old who was obsessed with per square foot price data on every property in a five square mile area. Remember, there were no internet sites for properties in 1994. This poor agent had to continually print out new reports for me and show me additional properties.

During my search, one of my colleagues in the PaineWebber internal audit department, Beth, and I struck up a conversation about my duplex search. It turned out that she had received a small inheritance and was also interested in purchasing a place. It would have taken nearly all of my savings to make the down payment on the type of place I wanted alone. And if I owned it alone, I would also have to shoulder the full responsibility of tenants. Long story short, I decided to partner with Beth on the purchase. She and I would each own 50%, and she would live in one half of the duplex with a roommate, and I would live in the other half with a roommate. We signed an agreement that would allow each of us to buy the other out under a particular set of circumstances.

With our agreement in place, we finally found the bargain we were looking for. I noticed on one of the realtor's printouts that a property I had been watching had dropped in price from $120k to $99k. I called our agent and found out that it was owned by an older woman who was retiring and was soon to leave for a cruise. She was dumping this property so she could pay for her trip. Instead of the going rate of $50 per square foot, she was willing to sell it for just over $41 per square foot. We called and secured a contract on the 2,400 square foot duplex immediately. We both *traded up* from our mass-market apartments to a much larger place with more conveniences around us, a nice patch of grass, and a more private setting.

During these first four-plus years out of college, I was very focused on *trading up in* all aspects of my life. I had *traded up* to a job with fewer hours, more pay, more social interaction, and a bigger view of the way business worked. I had also *traded up to a nicer* place to live that included homeownership rather than renting. While I had been raised in a home that put spiritual things above the material, I had not chosen what I considered a "ministry" track for my life. I pursued what I considered the American dream, bigger and better everything, with vigor. Extreme vigor.

While my pursuit of a bigger career, lifestyle, and bank account was in high gear, my spiritual life was firmly stuck in neutral. Similar to the printouts my real estate agent gave me a few years later, my father had sent me a printout of all the Presbyterian churches near my first apartment in Houston. Conveniently, there was one just a mile or so from my place named Memorial Drive Presbyterian Church. As I look back on it, I find it hard to describe the draw going to church had on me. For sure, one element was that I had a Pavlovian need to go—I had been trained to do so since birth. However, there was a second pull for me. I didn't like the feeling I had when I didn't go to church. I felt like I was missing something. Every single time I attended church, I felt a sense of peace and joy, and I liked getting that boost most Sundays.

I joined a Sunday school class, which was taught by a man named Peter Forbes. I instantly loved this guy. There would be about half a dozen of us 20-somethings who would show up, generally bleary-eyed from being out late the night before, wearing whatever we decided to throw on. And then there was Peter. Peter had grown up in Scotland and had that great Scottish accent that made everything he said sound important. He was about 50 years old with a solid handshake and eye contact that was as strong as his handshake. He would teach each class as if it was the last one that he would ever teach. I felt so unworthy to be the recipient of that level of preparation since my intensity for studying God's Word was nowhere close to his. Frankly, I don't remember one thing he said. But one thing I do remember vividly is the honor with which this humble, godly *businessman* behaved.

After receiving my Sunday booster shot of faith, I would prepare for the next week's battle. I remember having a discussion with one of my managers at Andersen as we were on our second eight-hour "shift" during busy season. I asked him what his priorities were in life. He told me he wanted to work hard, impress his bosses, and move up the ladder. He asked me what mine were. I told him I had been taught that you were to put God first, family second, and work third. He looked at me as if to say, "What planet are you from?" and as my words sank in, he appeared to smirk in a way that seemed to communicate, "You won't last long around here."

You see, I knew what to *say* from a Christian perspective, but I didn't do a great job of walking the walk. While my life had an undercurrent of faith, it was not bubbling to the surface. It was buried beneath my desire to live my life the way I wanted to live it.

I spent most of my time worrying about career advancement and my next date. Women were a huge focal point for me. In high school, I had the same girlfriend for two years. In college, I had the same God-fearing girlfriend for more than two years. They were both beautiful, God-fearing women. However, I was always looking to *trade up*. I was never satisfied. After college, other than my irregular Sunday morning church attendance and my occasional lip service about putting God first, there would have been little evidence that I knew Abraham from Anheuser Busch.

During the workweek, rather than having quiet time to commute with God, I had the opposite. I had an obsession with loud car stereo systems from the time I got my first car as a junior in college. Within five years of buying my first car, I had three car stereos stolen. I wasn't exactly subtle when driving around town. I think you could probably hear me (at least the crooks could!) a mile away. I justified my loud morning commute music by saying that it was my substitute for coffee. It certainly left no room for meaningful reflection.

During these years, my exploits as a singles tennis player continued. After college, free from the control of any high school or college coach who always subjected me to at least some doubles matches, I reveled in my freedom to play competitive singles *only*. I traveled all over Houston entering tournaments. *Ah, this is the life*, I thought to myself!

About a year into the PaineWebber audit job, I was ready to *trade up* again. It seemed to me that the financial advisors I met were having a lot more fun and making a lot more money than I was. I realized that being on the "expense" side of the ledger, where management was constantly figuring out how little they could pay to retain you, was not where I wanted to be. I wanted to be on the "revenue" side of the ledger, where they encouraged you to make as much money as possible because their bonuses were tied to your success.

However, I was drawn to the financial advisors' job description for more than the upscale income potential. I liked that the job required a "big picture" view of the world. An advisor needs to understand global economics and how large businesses operate. Additionally, although I'm not a pure extrovert (is any CPA?), I liked the idea that I could spend more time with people. In both audit jobs, I spent the majority of my time crunching numbers and writing reports. The financial advisor role seemed to offer me an ideal balance—one where I had unlimited upside income potential, a big-picture look at the world, interaction with people I could help, and just the right amount of number-crunching.

During my years as an auditor, I was constantly preparing for the next phase of my career. In those early years, I passed the CPA exam and obtained most of the licenses I would need to become a financial advisor. I was an auditor for PaineWebber for about two and a half years. During the last year of that job, after our team would finish the audit, I would ask to meet with what I viewed as the most successful advisors in each office I visited. From the information I had access to, I could tell who had the largest, cleanest businesses. I asked the branch managers to set up the interviews to put the advisors' minds at ease about having a private meeting with the auditor! The advisors were all very generous with their time and advice. Those meetings helped me craft a business plan for my own practice.

In 1994, I began researching where I should establish my practice. I was fortunate to know lots of branch managers and how the system worked. I narrowed my choices to three cities—San Diego, Chicago, and Houston. I eliminated St. Louis from the final three because I knew I needed a long list of prospects to go after. The only people I knew there were my parents' friends. And, while I liked the "halo effect" of visiting St. Louis and being thought well of as the son of Dr. Thomas, revered minister, I didn't want to trade on his name. I wanted to establish my own.

San Diego made the list because it's San Diego! Have you ever been there? I had done the audit of the PaineWebber office in San Diego and didn't want to leave. I fantasized about renting an apartment, buying a surfboard, and jumping into the ocean! However, I eliminated San Diego from the list for the same reason I took Mizzou off my college list. I knew it could be way *too* much fun, and I didn't want to lose focus on what I had to do to be successful. And being successful was *very* important to me. As a consequence, I still don't know how to surf!

I had also done audits of various Chicago branches. I really liked Chicago. It was a big city with lots of opportunities. Since it was only a few hundred miles from St. Louis, I would be closer to family. It had a large Andersen office and alumni network, which I intended to use as my niche market.

Eventually though, Houston won out. I already lived there. All of my business contacts, albeit limited, were there. I planned to market primarily to current and former Arthur Andersen employees, and the ones I knew were closer to Houston. Houston may not have had the physical beauty of San Diego, but at least it had warm enough weather to play tennis outside year-round. It also had bad enough weather occasionally to keep me inside working on my business, which was a huge priority for me.

The final decision came when one of the downtown Houston PaineWebber branch managers quickly agreed to start me at the same salary I had been making as an audi-tor—albeit declining quickly per the new financial advisor training program. This was nice because I knew that most new advisors took big pay cuts to enter the business for a shot at a bigger, long-term financial gain. When I told the Houston branch manager about the other cities I was con-sidering, he had a great line: "Look," he said, "Houston may not be beautiful, but it is a great place to do business. You will make so much money here that you will be able to travel any place you want on vacation." Man, he knew ex-actly what to say to me! I was sold. Houston is where I would *trade up* to my next career. It was an exciting but scary time. I wondered, "Do I really have what it would take to beat the odds and survive as a new advisor by my-self?"

When I started as an advisor on April 1, 1995, I was 26 years old. Most of my Andersen friends were on a very dif-ferent path. They were climbing the ladder of a large organ-ization's accounting department. A few of them went back to school to pursue an MBA. I had ruled out climbing the accounting ladder for the reasons I stated before—I wanted a broader view of business and the opportunity to use my communication skills. The possibility of an MBA intrigued me. I saw a path to a bigger view of business, like manage-ment consulting or investment banking, but the folks I knew in those jobs were very stressed out and didn't seem to control their own destiny. Unattractive qualities for a job a singles tennis player would consider! Additionally, I wasn't sure the money I would have to spend to leapfrog into a new career would be worth it. While there was more risk of failure, I was happy to have the risk "on my own racket" and throw myself into the financial advisor role.

Once I settled on Houston, the branch manager gave me an application that included a personality profile to see how I stacked up against the model the firm's psychologists had come up with to predict success in the business. Now, this worried me a little. I thought I was a good fit for the business, but who knows, maybe I was deluding myself? I knew this test was coming and had asked several successful advisors about it before I took it. Many of them told me they had not scored well initially, but their managers let them take it again, and they passed. The fact that several had failed it both scared me and encouraged me. It scared me because I wasn't positive this would work out for me, and it encouraged me because clearly all kinds of people actually succeeded in the business. My mind was put at some ease when one advisor gave me a useful tip about the test.

"They are testing for aggressive people who like to work by themselves," the advisor said.

"Oh, you mean like singles tennis players?" I asked.

"Exactly!" said the advisor.

I just smiled at the advisor and walked away. When I took the test, I answered the questions as though I was on the singles court playing for a Wimbledon title! When my scores came in, I got a call from my branch manager.

"The home office said you scored higher than anyone they have ever seen on this test," he said.

"Whew!" I said with a smile. *Let the games begin*, I thought. I was just happy to be past the hurdle of being approved for the job!

Trading Tip #2

Success is rarely a straight shot to the top—get used to it. It is usually a winding road with many twists and turns that often don't make sense at the time, but they are all combining to make you a better, wiser person. Just focus on the next step in front of you.

Question to Ponder

What are one or two events from your past that didn't seem very significant at the time, but now you see their importance in a new light?

LUPTON →

3

Breaking Out

 Success is the ability to go from one failure to another with no loss of enthusiasm.

—Winston Churchill

"I want you to make more money than me!" said the then-president of PaineWebber, Joe Grano. Mr. Grano was an intimidating figure. He was barrel-chested and looked the part of the retired military officer that he was.

His pronouncement came when I was in financial advisor training in New York for three weeks, shortly after passing the additional exams that were required for an advisor at PaineWebber.

"If you make more money than me, the company will make more profits, the stock will go up, and I'll do well also," he continued. And then he said something I will never forget.

"Look around this table," he said to the 30 or so of us who were in the room at the time. "Only a few of you will make it through this three-year training program," he said. "Who will it be?"

Images of a tennis tournament bracket came to my mind. *I know this game,* I thought.

I still remember his tips for how to succeed:

1. Scan the *Wall Street Journal* every day and especially be aware of any mention of PaineWebber.

2. Open an account every day. (He said that some days he'd call a distant uncle to open an account just so he could go home for the day saying he had met his goal.)

3. Don't be surprised if you lose your keys a lot. Be so focused on building a business that you lose track of everything else.

Grano's military background shone through clearly. This was a drill sergeant's pep talk. He didn't tell us to drop and give him push-ups, but he might as well have. This business would take everything we had just to make it past the first few years.

My first "office" was actually a cubicle on the 38th floor of the then-NCNB Building on Louisiana Street in Houston. I was surrounded by a few other trainees who were at various stages in the training program.

My game plan was simple. I would focus on a target market, build financial plans, invest the money, and be relentless. Armed with the alumni directory of the Houston Arthur Andersen office, I began calling these unsuspecting folks in the summer of 1995.

My pitch would go something like this: "Hi, this is Jeff Thomas, from PaineWebber. I understand you used to work at Andersen in Houston. So did I. Were you in Audit, Tax, or Consulting?" I would then ask a follow-up question, "When did you leave?"

Once they replied, I would drop the name of someone I knew that worked in their division near the same time they did. At that point, the person I was talking to knew we had some friends in common, so they were less likely to hang up on me. I would then offer to build them a financial plan and help them roll their Andersen 401(k) to an IRA. I would finish by asking permission to drop them a card and some information in the mail. I also asked if I could follow up once they received the information. Nearly everyone was gracious enough to allow me to do that. To this day, I joke that none of my clients have a last name past the letter "L" because I had enough going on after three years of making those calls that I quit calling halfway through the alphabet!

I basically followed a combination of Grano's advice and advice of the other successful advisors. My approach really boiled down to three simple principles:

1. Have a target market and a long list to call in that market.

2. Have a "unique value proposition" for said market.

3. Be relentless.

I watched many new advisors spend more energy complaining about the firm's flaws than on those basic principles. And, just as Grano predicted, 90% of them were gone within three years.

While full of rejection and often scary, this process was not too different from climbing the rankings as a tennis player. Every month, I received a report from the home office showing where I ranked nationally in my class of trainees. I battled it out near the top of the list and obsessed over making my goals and staying on top. I was not married, and I worked very long hours. I came into the office early and left late. Fear of failure and my competitive juices fueled me. The business was, indeed, a good fit for me as I had hoped. I got to look at the big global economic picture, be self-reliant, and interact with people to help them meet their goals.

Unfortunately, just nine months into this new adventure, in December of 1995, I got a distressed call from my mother. My father was in the hospital. He had suffered a brain hemorrhage. My sister and I were at his side on Christmas Day, and he passed away the next day. I had lost one of my biggest fans and my hero. Rather than spending a lot of time mourning his loss, I focused on only two things—my deathbed promise to take care of mom and my work. The long hours provided an escape from the pain of losing my father, the best "all-in" believer I knew.

As I called the 2,000 or so Andersen alumni, I knew I only needed about 100 to make a business for myself. I thought of my clients as a "flock"—much like my father thought of his parishioners. My unique value proposition to the ex-Andersen folks was that I was the "CFO's CFO." I told them I would take care of them as they climbed the corporate ladder. I asked them to refer me corporate business (401(k), cash management, stock option exercises) as well as any friends and family business. Many trusted me, and I took care of them the best way I knew how. To this day, I am grateful for their trust.

The Andersen target market worked for me. However, I wasted energy on plenty of other efforts that didn't pan out. One of them was my CPA referral plan. During training in Hoboken, New Jersey, we had been challenged to come up with a list of prospects in a target market and make some calls while we were there. The firm helped produce lists of prospects for us. I had a list produced of small CPA firms in Houston. My game plan was to call the lead partner at each of these firms with under 25 employees, get an appointment, and basically say, "I'm a CPA, you're a CPA—please refer me business." Apparently, this wasn't much of a value proposition, and the effort was an utter failure! I went to see quite a few of the lead partners at these various firms as they were kind enough to take the appointment. However, the CPA connection alone was not enough to build enough trust that they would instantly risk their reputation on a 26-year-old, brand new financial advisor. I got exactly zero new accounts from that effort.

My other great failure was in cold-calling people with whom I had nothing in common. In that era in Houston, there were quite a few financial advisors at Lehman Brothers who learned the business by cold-calling strangers. They had since dispersed all over the Street. A couple of them were in my office and would periodically hand me 3" x 5" note cards with names and telephone numbers on them. I believe they bought the lists from some source I had no clue about. I would call their cold calling cast-offs, and the results were predictable—that effort was unsuccessful for me and a complete waste of time. How desperate was I?

However, there was one guy about a year ahead of me in the training program who was great at cold-calling and was doing more business I was. He was the only other trainee who worked the same kind of hours I did. His name was Clay. We sat near each other in the "bullpen," which is what they called our section of cubicles. After I had been in the business for two years, I entered a partnership with Clay. He was impressed with my growth rate and offered me a 50/50 partnership. I agreed because the deal would be accretive to my income immediately, and I was impressed with Clay's work ethic and cold-calling skills.

Our partnership was mostly about camaraderie and having a back-up if we had to be out of the office. Eventually, Clay and I got our own offices. I still joke that the only real reason I got an office was that I was so loud in the bullpen that nobody else could hear themselves think when I was on the phone.

About a year into our partnership, Clay asked me if I thought we should talk to another advisor in the office, Risher, about working with us. I liked Risher. He was eight years older than I was and had eight more years of experience in the business. Risher was doing about the same in annual commissions as Clay and I were on track to do that same year. Risher's family had been in Galveston and Houston for many generations. He had a well-earned reputation in the community as a trustworthy guy who loved to talk about the markets. He had a great list of contacts that Clay and I believed we could convert to more business. That was the basic premise for the partnership—Risher would focus on the markets, Clay would do marketing, and I brought a client process that included financial planning. We struck a deal to be three equal partners.

Trading Tip #3

Trade a focus on results for a focus on the process. Understand that you are responsible for taking the right action and that God is in charge of the results. Change your scorecard.

Question to Ponder

What things, issues, or people are siphoning off your precious time and energy, which would be better spent on things you are responsible for and can control?

4

Forming a Bubble

Man plans, and God laughs.

—Yiddish Proverb

Bubbles are complicated things. One thing that makes them complicated is that they can go on for longer than anyone thinks is rational. An old trading quote that is often attributed to famed economist John Maynard Keynes says, "The market can remain irrational longer than you can remain solvent."[1]

By the year 2000, the S&P 500 Index was trading at a multiple of over 30 times earnings. This was the most expensive market in U.S. history. A lot of the excess was driven by the astronomically high valuations of technology stocks. The internet was becoming mainstream and being adopted by every business on the planet. The beginning of the boom happened when Netscape went public in 1995 (the same year I became a financial advisor). Companies would add ".com" to the end of their name just to garner a higher valuation. By late 1999, Initial Public Offerings (IPOs) were a dime a dozen. It seemed as though anyone who came up with a business plan that included making money on the internet could go public and raise hundreds of millions of dollars without any need for a history of actual earnings.

During this boom time for tech stocks, financial websites were not as commonplace. We still had Bloomberg terminals in our offices at PaineWebber. Several of my former Andersen clients would call me and ask me to compile financial information on their competitors for use in their own company's investor relations presentations. Being in Houston, most of our clients worked for companies in what was dubbed the "old economy." The old economy was any company that was not in the technology.

From 1998 to 2000, I vividly remember how the valuation statistics I compiled for these old economy companies differed from the tech sector valuations. The cash flow multiples of old economy companies were mostly in the single digits. When I would call my clients and review the information I prepared for them, the conversation would inevitably turn to a comparison of high-flying tech stock valuations. I remember one client asking me, "What is Yahoo trading for today?"

I remember answering, "Five million times today's eyeballs!" We would share a big laugh! I kid you not—a "legitimate" valuation statistic in those days was a count of how many people looked at an internet site in a day. Earnings and positive cash flow were considered dusty relics of the old economy.

I tried to get every client possible out of tech stocks in 1998. I was deathly afraid that those stocks were going to come tumbling down at any moment. I didn't want to have a penny left invested in that sector when it happened. Unbelievably, the boom went on for another two years! When

I tell the story of rushing to get out of tech stocks in 1998, it sounds like a great story. After all, we helped save people a lot of money by doing so, right? While we did limit losses for clients, I don't remember that as a time of celebration. I remember it mostly as a time of pain.

It was a *long* two years from the time I started getting people out of tech until the actually sell-off began. While I believed the facts of overvaluation were indisputable, what I expected to happen, a collapse in the sector, did not happen on the timetable I expected it to. During that time, I would periodically get unsolicited calls from clients to buy tech stocks. I couldn't talk everyone out of it. For two years, they generally made big money on those trades while I played the role of Chicken Little, squawking that the sky was falling.

I have to admit—I lost a lot of sleep during those two years. Some clients and many prospective clients couldn't resist telling me how great their internet mutual funds were doing at E-Trade (several of my clients finally got tired of my sighs of frustration at their desire to buy tech stocks and resorted to opening on-line accounts to do so). We made clients an average of 15-20% per year in 1998 and 1999 with over-weights in dirt-cheap financial stocks that had been left for dead in the old economy while regularly hearing about internet funds doing over 80% annually. My advice was underperforming massively, and I was feeling the pressure and beginning to think that maybe *I* was the crazy one. Although I didn't do it for clients, I personally shorted some of the most ridiculously overpriced internet stocks only to have to cover my trades at a loss as the stocks continued to climb to ridiculous heights. These personal losses rubbed salt in my wounds.

Near the peak of the tech bubble in 1999, Clay suggested we add a fourth partner, Greg, who had been a trader in New York. Shortly after the trader was added to our team, Clay left the team to raise capital for a start-up tech company.

These were crazy times. Thanks to the frothy market (people who called to buy stocks, unsolicited), productive partners, and sheer hard work (more like obsession), my revenue continued to climb. My production didn't mirror Netscape's moonshot of rising six-fold within five months of its August 1995 IPO, but it was still pretty good. I was able to go from $0 to $1mm in production within my first five years. My inferiority complex for not having gone to graduate school began to fade. At age 31, I was making more money than the new partners at the large accounting firm I came from, and my peers there wouldn't make partner for another five years. I was making over 10 times what I had made my last year as an internal auditor. I had *traded up*! While I understood the importance of taking care of clients and that serving them was the key to my success, I was still keeping score for myself by how much money I was making. I was always working to *trade up* to the next level of production. I remember a sales manager telling me that doing $500k in production changed your life, but that doing $1mm made it twice as good! *I bought it.*

While my income grew, I kept my expenses low. All I did was work. Thanks to the purchase of the duplex and the rent from my roommate, even my home provided positive cash flow. In 1998, I decided to splurge and buy a new suit. I went to Neiman Marcus and perused the suit rack. While I was browsing, I saw it—the same tan suit I had seen on the guy I sold the discounted commercial properties to in D.C.! I gleefully paid $1,200 for the silk-blend Armani suit. That suit felt spectacular. I had made it; I had *traded up*. Or so I thought. I went back and bought several suits there over the next few years. But somehow none of them gave me the same thrill that first tan suit did. Soon, that suit, along with my hubris, wore thin.

During this time, I was obsessed with the markets, my clients, and building the business. However, my spiritual life continued on cruise control. I attended the same church I had attended from the beginning of my Houston adventure with the same lukewarm enthusiasm. I made it to church 75% of the time, but I was 25% engaged. I loved the shot in the arm Sunday mornings gave me. I would be on a spiritual high all day from the Sunday school and worship experience. The sugar rush faded as the workweek extended. But I always felt the pull and power of the church and God. It was a comfortable, familiar place, but I was stuck in neutral as far as my spiritual growth was concerned. In reality, my true god was my business and bank account, although I would never have admitted it back then.

While the markets were peaking, so was my tennis game. I was working in Heritage Plaza, a 53-story skyscraper on the edge of downtown Houston. Just a block away was the Metropolitan Club (the "Met") that had 10 indoor tennis courts. I was back to playing tennis indoors, just like I had done since I was a kid in St. Louis. Only this time, I was playing indoors to avoid the heat instead of the snow! I still enjoyed competing on the tennis court as much as I did in the office.

During 1997, while I was talking to one of my ex-Andersen and fellow PK friends, Walter, he invited me to a luncheon that another local church was putting on as a workplace ministry outreach. I vaguely remember the speakers talking about how they integrated their faith with their work. I, however, will never forget that luncheon for another reason. Walter had brought one of his co-workers, Dolly Dawson, with him. That moment changed my life forever. When I saw her, my heart leapt. She was stunningly beautiful. She had a bright smile and was impeccably dressed, and she made me wish I had on my tan suit!

I made sure that we sat next to each other at that luncheon. We shared the same sense of humor. We cracked jokes and only half-listened to the presentation. I discovered that her father was also a minister and that she had also worked at Andersen but had left before I had arrived. We exchanged phone numbers and began talking regularly. I discovered that she had been widowed at the age of 29 and had a four-year-old daughter from her marriage. While I was certainly interested in being more than just friends from the beginning, marrying a woman with a four-year-old was not part of the plan I had for my life. She did not show much dating interest, either. She was busy with her daughter and was four years older than me.

Helping her with her financial planning and investments was a great excuse for me to stay in touch with Dolly. I met her daughter, Ally, and was surprised at how I felt about her. I knew nothing about kids, but I loved Ally right away. She was the cutest, happiest four-year-old I had ever met. Not that I had met a lot, but she was special to me. Her infectious smile lit up the room even back then. One of the things I will always remember about that time was the way Dolly presented herself and Ally. I had been around a few other single mothers, and they all seemed to be apologetic about their kids. Dolly was different. She acted as though Ally was a bonus to any relationship she might have.

As my feelings grew for Dolly and Ally, my objections to dating a single mother went up in smoke. I finally asked Dolly on a date. On our first date, somehow, we ended up playing pool. Two ex-Andersen, PKs who grew up playing pool in their parents' houses—what were the odds? The rest, as they say, is history.

The following year, I asked Dolly to marry me, and six months later, in the spring of 1999, we said, "I do," with six-year-old Ally as the only attendant at our wedding. I gave Ally a heart necklace during the ceremony, and she stole the show!

Our wedding ceremony was at West University United Methodist Church, where Dolly had long been a member. I always thought that if I ever got married, we would likely end up at a Presbyterian church. After all, I had the PK trump card in my hip pocket, right? Well, God has a sense of humor because He brought me a wife that had five generations of Methodist ministers on *both* sides of her family. I had been trumped to the tenth degree! So, can you guess what denomination I am part of? Correct. I became a Methodist!

During 1997, Beth, the co-owner of my duplex, moved to New York, and I bought out her interest in the duplex in accordance with our agreement. Two years later, just before Dolly and I got married, I sold the place during an up-turn in the real estate market to a church school that was catty-corner to the property. Dolly and I pooled our resources and bought a single-family home nearby. I had *traded up* from a duplex to a single-family home in one of the most exclusive neighborhoods in Houston.

Having found Dolly was as much a relief as it was exciting. I finally found a beautiful woman who shared the same worldview and liked to have fun. I was thrilled to end my effort to continually *trade up* in that area of my life. I had *traded up* to marriage.

The stock market continued to soar for the remainder of 1999. Our newest partner, Greg, started meeting with other brokerage firms who were interested in having us join them. Risher and I were initially reluctant to meet with anyone as we had our heads set on building a business. However, we finally relented and met with representatives from Morgan Stanley Dean Witter (MSDW). Dean Witter had purchased Morgan Stanley in 1997 and had built a powerful platform. Risher and I were impressed. The scale of the combined organizations was a draw for us. In early 2000, PaineWebber's CEO, Don Marron, continually stated that PaineWebber was unlikely to merge with a global bank and scale. Risher and I liked MSDW's strategy better and began to entertain a move. The money MSDW was offering didn't hurt either.

Risher and I had a lot of long talks before we made the final decision to move. One of the central ones was the risk that Greg might not be able to join us. We all knew that Greg's short list of clients was quasi-institutional and might have some loyalty to PaineWebber.

The dot-com bubble burst, numerically, on March 10, 2000, when the technology-heavy NASDAQ Composite index peaked at 5,048.62 (intra-day peak 5,408.60), more than double its value just a year before.

Risher, Greg, and I planned to move to MSDW on Friday, March 31, 2000, just three weeks after the peak of the NASDAQ bubble. In those days, it was traditional to switch brokerage firms on a Friday afternoon, so that the firm you were leaving didn't have time to pass out your accounts to other advisors until the following week. It slowed those advisors from calling your clients and trying to talk them into staying at the firm you were leaving. I found the cloak and dagger process to be a bit ridiculous. Even though most big firms considered the clients you brought in to be "their" clients, everyone in the industry knew that 90% of clients typically followed the advisor, not the firm. Fortunately, that was the case for Risher and me. We furiously called all of our clients, and the great majority followed us to our new firm.

The move did have one large casualty—our partner Greg. Just a few months before our move, we had hired a new assistant who had apparently tipped off our PaineWebber branch manager that we were planning to leave. This allowed PaineWebber management to call all of Greg's institutional clients and ask them to stay. Greg was forced to stay behind while Risher and I fulfilled our promise to move to MSDW.

When Risher and I landed at MSDW, we felt like we had *traded up.* We had a larger platform for our clients, had gotten a nice paycheck to move, and had a more stable partnership with just the two of us and two assistants.

Trading Tip #4 – Trade Playing Singles for Playing Doubles.

Understand that life is a team sport. Once you know your mission, concentrate your time on that and find a team to do the things that aren't your strengths.

Question to Ponder

Who would be the best person in your world for you to begin drawing from or even partnering with? What keeps you from taking that step?

---

[1] R.F. Harrod, *The Life of John Maynard Keynes* (New York: W.W. Norton & Company, Inc., 1951).

5

Breaking Down

I've missed more than 9,000 shots in my career. I've lost almost 300 games. 26 times, I've been trusted to take the game-winning shot and missed. I've failed over and over and over again in my life. And that is why I succeed.

—Michael Jordan

No bubble lasts forever. You don't know when the peak of a bubble is until you look back with the benefit of hindsight.

When we moved to MSDW in March of 2000, the NASDAQ Index had risen to over 5,000, and we knew the tech sector was wildly overpriced. What we didn't know was that our move corresponded with what was to be the absolute peak of the NASDAQ bubble. The 5,000 level was not seen again for 15 years.

Right after our arrival at the new firm, the markets began to crumble. The Dow Jones Industrial Average (the "Dow") peaked on January 14, 2000 intraday at 11,750. It bottomed on September 24, 2002, at 7,286 a drop of nearly 38%. The NASDAQ's volatility was even more dramatic.

After peaking at 5,048, it bottomed the same day as the Dow at 1,114—an epic drop of nearly 80%.

Now, you might think that since I had been advising clients to stay away from tech stocks for two years, this would be a celebratory time for me. However, with the rest of the market getting caught up in the crash, that was not the case. There was no place to hide during that bear market.

The excesses of the 2000 bubble came home to roost all across the country--not just in Silicon Valley. Houston certainly was not exempt. We were home to Enron, which became the poster child for corporate malfeasance. Enron's demise also led to the demise of my old firm, Arthur Andersen.

In 2002, Andersen collapsed after being found guilty of criminal charges relating to the firm's handling of the auditing of Enron. The verdict was subsequently overturned by the Supreme Court, but the damage to its reputation prevented it from returning as a viable business.

The demise of Andersen was an emotional and financial hit to a lot of my friends and former colleagues. Everyone had been so proud to work at the Firm and never dreamt it could disappear. When I joined Andersen in 1990, it had a stellar reputation thanks to a strong tradition of excellence.

With that kind of history and knowing the quality of the people I was surrounded by at that Firm, it was amazing that a scandal from the Houston office took down the entire company. I felt especially bad for my old colleagues who were still at the Firm when it went under.

Andersen and Enron had some spectacularly talented employees. Most of them found productive new work environments in fairly short order. However, the concept of security and trust in large institutions had forever been shattered for me and countless others in Houston and throughout the country.

Fortunately, our clients were as well-positioned as could be expected during this time. That allowed their portfolios to hang in pretty well during a nasty downturn. That fact, in turn, allowed our team's revenue to remain fairly stable. We had dropped somewhat during the natural transition to MSDW and dropped some more due to the bursting of the tech bubble. No one was calling in to do trades much anymore, but, overall, we held our own in terms of business revenue.

However, it certainly wasn't a comfortable time, personally or professionally. The discomfort of tumultuous markets carried over into other areas of life for me. As the markets were topping in late 1999, other seeds of discomfort were being planted. In September of 1999, only months after becoming the father of a second-grader, I vividly remember one particular car ride after church. As we turned from University Boulevard north onto Buffalo Speedway, I remember looking in the rearview mirror at that cute, little Ally and asking her, "What did you learn in Sunday School?"

"I made this," Ally replied and held up a picture she had drawn.

Now, there is a great reason I could never make it as a professional poker player. I have a terrible poker face. This was the fourth Sunday in a row that Ally heard me ask her that same question. She could see from my furrowed brow that her consistent answer of "I made this" was not satisfying me.

All I was looking for was an answer such as "God loves me" or "Jesus was God's son." Was that too much to ask from her Sunday School teachers?

As my brow began to furrow again in frustration with her volunteer teachers, Ally delivered a line that I will never forget: "Daddy, maybe you and I should do a Bible study together."

The seven-year-old delivered a lightning bolt! The truth nearly knocked me into the next lane: it was my responsibility to teach my daughter about faith, not the Sunday school teachers'. My mental BB gun shot at her teachers, bounced off the trash can, and hit me square between the eyes!

Out of the mouths of babes, I thought.

I knew that interchange was a direct message from God. I had always seen church as a place that was supposed to spiritually feed my family. While I was the *son* of a pastor, *I* was not a pastor. *I* was not in ministry. *I* wanted to benefit from the wisdom of people who were. What was *I* supposed to do now?

Well, I had no idea how to teach the Bible to a second grader—or anyone else for that matter. It was still early in the school year, and I had enrolled in a Disciple Bible Study at our church that met on Sunday evenings. I was just a few weeks into the study. One of our pastors was leading it. I had joined the study because God had already put it on my heart to learn more about His Word. In fact, over the last year or so, I had questioned whether I even wanted to study the Bible. Were the contents even true? I wasn't sure. Did I believe everything I heard in church just because I had been raised to believe it?

To answer those questions, I searched for books that I thought would honestly address the question of the authenticity of the Bible. I landed on a book called *The Case for Christ* by Lee Strobel. I liked the premise of the book. Lee had been a card-carrying atheist and an investigative reporter. He was dismayed when his wife started going to church. In an effort to debunk Christianity the way he had exposed the mob in Chicago, he threw himself into looking for cracks in the story. As he tells it, he ended up convincing himself that the Bible was historically accurate and became a Christ-follower.

The book was so well researched and went so deep into the validity of the Bible that I only got about halfway through it before I cried "uncle!" The evidence for the Bible's authenticity seemed irrefutable to me, too. This was a big turning point. Even though I had accepted Christ as a 13-year-old fresh out of confirmation class, I started to have a strong desire to more deeply pursue a relationship with Christ. However, I was embarrassed about how little I knew about the Bible. Here I was, the son of a man who had a doctorate in this stuff, and all I knew were a bunch of fairly disjointed Bible stories, much like my seven-year-old daughter. Osmosis didn't work for a deep understanding of the Bible. In my quest for that understanding, I had signed up for that Disciple Bible Study.

When Ally's lightning-bolt question hit me, it threw me into a tailspin. Could I translate the weekly studies I had just begun to her? That seemed too difficult. Were there books we could study together? How was I going to find the right resources? I knew I had to do something. I didn't know what it was. I prayed for an answer.

The answer came quickly. Literally, within two weeks of Ally asking me that question, Risher strode into my office one morning and said, "Hey Jeff, I'm starting a Bible study class for second graders through an organization called Bible Study Fellowship (BSF). However, fathers have to show up and do a study of their own the same night on the same chapters. You will probably need to help Ally with her homework in the class before you both arrive each week. Are you interested?"

"Are you freaking kidding me? Yes!" I responded. I think Risher was shocked at my answer. He asked lots of people to join BSF and rarely got that kind of enthusiastic answer!

This was one of my first experiences where my prayers were answered almost immediately. That was a powerful moment for me. I felt that God was giving me a wink of encouragement for my families' newfound zeal to learn more about Him. I have learned in the years since that the more I align with the path God has for me, the more I experience "God moments" like this where He reveals Himself to me.

Ally and I spent the next two years studying the Bible together every week during the school year. I had *traded up* from a passive parent to an active teacher. I was also *trading up* from lukewarm church attender to red-hot believer. God responded to my leaning into Him in a big way. I couldn't get enough of His wisdom. I had always harbored a strong desire to know how the world worked in all ways. At work, I was constantly learning how the global economic system worked. Now, for the first time, I felt like I was able to put the spiritual puzzle together, too. It was like I had been given all of the pieces thanks to my upbringing and exposure to Christ, but I hadn't engaged in the act of actually snapping the pieces of the puzzle into place. Studying the Bible helped me understand the spiritual world better, and I ate it up.

While the markets were going straight down, my faith was going straight up! As a "process guy," BSF's style suited me. The homework each week included a few passages of scripture to read each day with a follow-up question or two about the days' reading. Every Sunday night, I would help Ally with her BSF homework on the same verses I was studying during the week. Every Monday night, Ally and I would go to our separate small groups (I was in a class with about 10 men of similar age) and hear about how others had interpreted the week's lessons. I always did the homework because BSF had a rule that you couldn't speak in class unless you had done the homework—and I couldn't stand the idea of not being able to participate!

However, I generally had an arrogant attitude walking into class. I had done the homework, and I usually felt like I had interpreted the point of the reading well. Why did I need to hear what these other people thought? Didn't I already know the answers? It was amazing to me how consistently I walked in with that attitude and how consistently I walked out with a fresh perspective from the others. This non-denominational class was filled with men of all races, from all parts of Houston, who belonged to all kinds of different churches. We had men who ranged from business titans to city bus drivers in the same classroom. I learned from all of them.

After the small group time, we would assemble in the sanctuary of the host church, and about 300 of us would listen to a 45-minute lecture on the scripture we had just studied. After the lecture, on our way out the doors, we would get our homework for the next week that included several pages of professional notes on the history and common interpretations of the verses we had studied the week before. This process of reading the scriptures, writing my interpretations, listening to my peers, and studying the professional notes gave me the foundation of biblical knowledge I so desperately craved.

At that time, BSF had a seven-year cycle that took one through approximately 90% of the Bible. I went to that study for seven years in a row, a total sponge for God's Word. I had always craved an understanding of the big picture—both in business and in life. I had finally found a career that compensated me for studying global economics and had found what I believed was the source of true wisdom in life—God's Word!

Not only did BSF help build my understanding of the Bible, but I got to do it with both of my girls. In 2001, Dolly and I welcomed our daughter Sophie into the world. When she was old enough, I started taking her to BSF as well.

BSF provided a forum for me to communicate and discuss true wisdom with them. I had always appreciated the example my parents had set in their faith, and it was probably a good thing that they didn't thump the Bible too hard in front of me, as I might have rebelled as so many other PKs have done. I had a strong desire to understand how the world worked and had to research it for myself. What I discovered was a confirmation that my parents had tapped into the right source for their hope and a deeper understanding of what drew my dad to the pulpit.

This seven-year period from 2000 to 2007 was a wonderful time of spiritual growth for me, but it also revealed some "stinkin' thinkin'" I had adopted.

Before I studied the Bible so intently, I thought I was a pretty good person by the world's standards. If you listed out the Ten Commandments, I would have told you that I kept them all—at least better than most people. Studying the Bible, ironically, made me feel much worse about myself. I had heard people talk about the Bible being like a mirror that you hold up to yourself. I never really understood what they meant until I started to study it so closely.

In reading God's Word, I learned about how high His standards were. The more I learned, the clearer it became to me that I did not measure up. It was a humbling discovery. I was not nearly as good a person as I had built myself up to be in my own mind.

This lack of satisfaction in my performance had a huge impact on my business. In 2005, I was five years deep into studying the Bible daily and 10 years deep into my career as a financial advisor.

While the market turmoil did take a short-term toll on the revenue of our practice, we had been planning for such a downturn with our clients, so they weren't immensely impacted. What was less expected was the downturn in my own satisfaction with the way I was performing my job. I had always prided our business on being "a safe place for people to go" to find trustworthy help for their financial planning and investment needs. I even thought of my clients as "my flock," similar to the one my dad had in his church membership, as I referenced earlier. In a business with a reputation for manipulative sales, I tried to be transparent with clients about exactly how the business worked—what the fees were, how I got compensated, etc.

At that time, a very small percentage of advisors at the large wirehouses ran financial plans for clients. They generally jumped to an investment discussion as quickly as possible. However, I had focused on financial planning from the very beginning. I had learned, as an auditor, how to build a work program to complete each engagement. I took that same principle to my financial advisory practice. I built financial plans for every client who would allow me to follow that process. I felt I was doing them a great service by helping them find out if they were on track with their goals. Those goals were mainly funding retirement and college educations for their children. Once we were on the same page about the financial plan, I would discuss an investment plan I felt would get them there.

I spent 10 years doing the same three things—marketing, planning, and investing. The business had grown to where I was a success by most of the world's measures, and I had met my personal financial goals. I had *traded up* from an apartment to a great house, from a compact car to a luxury sedan, and from a discontent single person to a happily married man. As a parent, I helped my daughter *trade up* to private school. As a family, we began taking international vacations instead of just domestic ones. At Morgan Stanley, I was quickly climbing the national leaderboard of producers.

Besides doing my job at work and supporting my family, on the surface, I was successful outside of work as well. I was keeping fit, playing tennis with a group of other successful men, and I was active at church. At least active in the way people who weren't "in ministry" were active—as part of various committees. At one time or another, I served on the Board of Stewards, the Staff Parish Relations Committee, the Finance Committee, and even taught Sunday school occasionally.

While everything seemed great on the outside, I was in turmoil on the inside. I was reading scripture verses like the following that disturbed me:

> For from him and through him and to him are all things… (Rom. 11:36)

> You are not your own; you were bought at a price… (1 Cor. 6:19-20)

> You may say to yourself, "My power and the strength of my hands have produced this wealth for me." But remember the LORD your God, for it is he who gives you the ability to produce wealth... (Deut. 8:17-18)

> The earth is the Lord's, and everything in it, the world, and all who live in it. (Psa. 24:1)

> "The silver is mine, and the gold is mine," declares the LORD Almighty. (Haggai 2:8)

> His master replied, "Well done, good and faithful servant! You have been faithful with a few things; I will put you in charge of many things. Come and share your master's happiness!" (Matt. 25:21)

In 2005, it was as if every Bible verse that I read screamed at me about the idea of "stewardship" versus "ownership." I have joked many times that if I even read "Jesus wept" during that year, I would have found a way to interpret something about stewardship from it.

God was getting my attention. I had believed all my life that I was in charge. If I studied hard, I got good grades. If I got good grades, I got into a good college. If I worked hard in college, I would get a good job. If I found a job I enjoyed and worked hard at it, I would have financial success. In December every year, I would write my business plan for the next year and ask God to help me make it happen.

These verses were making it clear to me that I was not in charge. I had heard the phrase "God owns it all" before, but that was a distant platitude for me. Yes, I knew God created the earth and everything, but while He was busy with the big picture, I believed I had to make things happen for myself down here. The reality was sinking in that even though I was making my own agenda, relying on myself for outcomes, and patting myself on the back for my achievements, none of that would have been possible if God didn't create me in the first place, give me the parents I had, place me in this country at this time, and give me the physical and mental attributes to succeed.

For the first time in my life, I understood the true meaning of the story of the rich young ruler in the Bible. You probably know the story.

It was near the end of Jesus' ministry, and this guy sincerely drops to his knees before Christ and asks what he needs to do to get to heaven. Christ tries to let him off the hook and says, "You know the commandments," and starts ticking them off.

The guy interrupts and says, "I've done all that stuff since I was a kid."

Then Jesus comes with the knockout punch and says, "You still lack one thing," and proceeds to tell him to give everything to the poor and follow him. You probably know the rest of the story—the young ruler chooses his possessions over Jesus' commands.

Growing up, I never liked that story. To me, it reinforced the idea that to be truly "all in" for God, you had to sell everything and move to Africa. Well, I didn't want to do that, so I concluded that I clearly wasn't "called" to be in full-time ministry.

As I read this story again in 2005, a new revelation came to me. Jesus isn't trying to tell us that we *all* need to sell everything as I had believed for so long. He is telling us that he wants us to prioritize Him above all else. I finally understood that, in this story, he was looking into the heart of the person he was talking to *specifically*. The rich young ruler tied his identity to his possessions. Jesus simply wanted him to let go of whatever was getting in the way of allowing Jesus to lead. He was inviting the Rich Young Ruler to *trade up*! I asked myself what I was holding onto that was getting in the way of my relationship with Jesus? *Yikes*, I thought, *lots of things*. My desire for self-reliance began to melt away as I realized there was no such thing.

During the time when this revelation was sinking in for me, Dolly and I attended a fundraiser for Child Advocates, a non-profit she has been involved with for many years that trains volunteers to shepherd abused and neglected kids to a safe home. At the event, I purchased an auction item that was a one-foot-tall sculpture called "The Self- Made Man." It is a statue of a man swinging a hammer, attempting to form himself out of a block of iron—an impossible task. Around the same time, I bought a photograph by Michael Belk called "Daily Bread," where he shows Jesus sitting at a table with one piece of bread while a man in a suit stands a few feet from him clutching several loaves of bread refusing to make eye contact with Jesus. Both of these art pieces sit in my office to remind me of who is in charge.

"So," I asked myself, "if I'm not in charge, and Jesus is, what does that mean for my life?"

The answer to that question completely changed the direction of my career.

All this time, I had been acting as though I was this great singles player. When, in fact, God was quietly playing doubles with me, setting me up to hit easy overheads and waiting for me to acknowledge Him. He wasn't just my partner—he had created the entire game and the venue. He had built the stadium, painted the lines, taught me how to serve, put me on the court with Him, and invited me to play! To be truly successful, all I had to do was to acknowledge His sovereignty, use the skills He had given me, and follow His lead. This was a major breakthrough in my thinking! In a new and wonderful way, the pressure was now off. He was in charge, and I was just there to steward the gifts He gave me in a way He would appreciate and delight in.

My mind immediately turned to the financial advisory practice that I now realized He had provided for me. With this new understanding of stewardship, I began wondering how I needed to change the ways I was currently running *His* business.

Trading Tip #5

Trade ownership for stewardship. Understand that God owns it all, including your business. This takes the pressure off of you.

Question to Ponder

Have you ever thought of stewardship as "freeing"? What change(s) could you make in your business to experience this truth?

6

Building a New Base

Life is either a daring adventure or nothing.
Security is mostly a superstition.

—Helen Keller

Armed with my new recognition that God truly does own it all, and feeling relieved that I was no longer in charge, I wondered, "Now what?"

I finally understood what it meant to be "all in" with God, mentally and spiritually. Before gaining this fuller understanding of ownership versus stewardship, I had defined being "all in" for God as a profession, either as a minister or a missionary. For the first time in my life, I realized that God wasn't nearly as interested in my profession as he was in my commitment to Him. The issue wasn't occupation but consecration.

This newly discovered truth began transforming my heart and mind, but I wasn't sure how to turn it into action.

During this time, I mentioned my dilemma to a fellow believer and colleague in my office, Pat Combs. Pat was a relatively new advisor in our branch, with an impressive background. He played baseball at Rice and Baylor Universities and had been drafted in 1988 as a first-round pick by the Philadelphia Phillies. After a meteoric rise to the big leagues, he was plagued with arm problems and finally had to give up his professional baseball career after eight years. Following a short stint as a staff member for the Fellowship of Christian Athletes (FCA) and a seven-year career as an executive coach, he joined Morgan Stanley.

Now, I rarely hung out with other advisors. In my singles player's mind, I thought it was, in general, a waste of time. After all, I was all about growing the business, and other advisors weren't going to open an account with me. However, there were a few exceptions. Pat was one of them. We got along well because of our similar backgrounds. He was an incredibly hard worker, and I understood his competitive nature. I also liked the fact that he had a strong faith and wasn't afraid to talk about it.

I shared with Pat my dilemma about what to do with my newfound understanding of stewardship, and he gave me a book called *Halftime*, by Bob Buford. I could not put it down! It told the story of Bob Buford's path from success as a business person in the first half of his life to his search to find significance in the second half of his life. He, too, wanted to be "all in" for God but did not feel like his highest and best use was to move to Africa.

Bob found his calling in applying all of the things he had learned in the first half of his life to creating an organization that helped other high-capacity believers find their callings. Often those callings were to use their business skills in a slightly new way. No, let me rephrase that—a *radically* new way. As I turned the pages, the light bulb went on, and the scales fell from my eyes. I saw that I could be "all in" for God without drawing a paycheck from a non-profit. What a relief! Bob's book gave me permission to look for meaning within a business context. At the end of *Halftime*, Bob referenced another book he had written called *Game Plan*. In *Game Plan*, I walked through a process to figure out the unique skills and experiences God had given me, and I was challenged to think anew about how to apply those assets to honor God in the second half of my life.

The result of this process was a three-point "game plan" for the second half of my life. Here's what I wrote as my game plan:

1. Help out with stewardship at church.

2. Implement biblical principles into my advice to clients.

3. Once I consistently and effectively accomplished point two above, help other advisors do the same.

Reading those books and creating this game plan was a "burning bush" moment for me. I had always wished that God would speak to me more clearly and tell me exactly what to do, as He did with Moses and other prophets. However, I discovered He had been doing that for years, but I wasn't listening very well. By finally studying His Word more deeply and praying more fervently—essentially engaging with Him at a new level—He revealed to me a new understanding of my proper relationship with Him. More importantly, I was seeing for the first time that I didn't have to draw my paycheck from a non-profit to be "all-in" for Him. Finally, He gave me an explicit track to run on.

I was incredibly excited! As I wrote those three goals on the paper in front of me, I truly felt like God was guiding my pencil, especially as I wrote out point three. As I mentioned earlier, I barely even talked with other advisors up to that point in my career. Now, a third of my game plan was to work with them? That sounded like playing doubles. I knew *that* had to be God's idea!

This new game plan gave me a renewed sense of purpose. I felt like my mission in life had finally become clear.

By leaning into God through prayer and Bible study and being in relationship with other believers, He had shown me the truth that He owned it all. He also taught me about the proper place money has in a person's life. I learned that Jesus spoke about money and possessions more than he spoke about heaven and hell combined! There are over 2,400 verses in the Bible about money and possessions. One of the key verses I had learned was Matthew 6:24:

> No one can serve two masters; for either he will hate the one and love the other, or else he will be loyal to the one and despise the other. You cannot serve God and money.

God could have picked a myriad of things to use in this verse that compete with Him for our attention (other gods, relationships, recreation, etc.), but He chose money. Why? Because God knew that was **the** most common problem. It dawned on me that this wisdom about money's proper place in one's life was not commonly taught. I was in the business of counseling people about money, and I never brought it up. That was convicting. I was on the front lines of a war for people's hearts, and I had been blind to it!

Thanks to God's wisdom and Bob Buford's mentorship through his books, I woke up and realized that I was an infantryman in this war. I wanted to find a way to engage in helping people understand the proper place money has in their lives. God's three-point game plan for my life became my marching orders to be "all-in" for Him, without drawing a check from a non-profit.

As you might expect, some parts of carrying out my three-point plan were easier than others. Helping out with the stewardship campaign at church came naturally—I had a ready-made platform there to plug into. I was excited to communicate this newfound wisdom of mine concerning money and possessions. I think my pastor was a little shocked to have someone *volunteer* in this area! I enjoyed sharing my story of revelation that God owns it all.

The idea of implementing Biblical wisdom into my financial advisory practice would also come naturally, I thought. For the first time in my life, I realized that God could use me within the platform He had already given me. I could be in full-time ministry in the workplace—what a concept! I could be just as much a missionary as the family working in New Guinea or my dad, the pastor. My whole paradigm was changing. I was morphing from a passive, cultural Christian standing on the sidelines, rooting on the "all-in" believers, like ministers and missionaries, into a player on the field with them. I had spent my entire life thinking that since I didn't feel a "call" to be a pastor, I was not called to be in ministry. I had been wrong about this all my life! I was called to be in ministry all along, just not the way I thought!

The third point of the plan was something I would deal with later. Before I helped any other advisors, I had to figure out how to lovingly tell my own clients that their money wasn't really theirs! Ha! That didn't sound like a very easy sales pitch! Frankly, I had no idea how to change the conversation at work.

For years, when clients would engage me, I would build a financial plan that would tell them when they could securely retire and live on their money without reliance on anyone else. Now, I realized, there were three major things wrong with this approach.

First of all, as I mentioned above, the money wasn't really "theirs," but His. So, I needed to change my vocabulary and approach to help them realize they were stewards, not owners. We were to figure out what He wanted us to do with his money.

Secondly, there is no such thing as financial security (or any other kind of security, for that matter) apart from Him. One of my favorite expressions is "there is no safer place in life than in the will of God." If God wants to take away what He gave us, he can do that at any time. Just ask Jonah how things went for him when God told him to deliver a message he didn't want to deliver. He ended up in a whale. Talk about not being in charge!

Thirdly, in my study of the Bible, I could find no references to retirement, yet that's what I was implicitly encouraging. I needed to find a way to engage clients in a discussion of how to "re-tire" (add new tread) rather than retire. I needed to find a way to encourage them to use their God-given talents even if they left their current employer.

While all those changes *sounded* great, I had been doing things the same *old* way for 10 years. That was certainly long enough for me to get stuck in my ways. Additionally, the approach I had taken up to that point had resulted in fantastic "production" by the way the world defined that word. I wondered if this would be a disaster for me—like a mini version of the Coca-Cola disaster in 1985 when they rolled out "New Coke." Everyone asked, "Why mess with something that was working?"

I did *not* know how to change the conversation. I used Google to search phrases like "the Bible and money" and discovered millions of results that I could never sort through. I ordered every book I could find on Amazon about values-based planning. I found nothing that helped. My poor wife began complaining about the giant stack of books accumulating in the house on the topic. However, I was committed to figuring out how to deepen the conversation with clients.

One day during this period, I walked into my branch manager's office and told him about my new game plan.

"Shawn, I feel like God is telling me to have a deeper conversation with clients about money and the proper place it has in their lives. I know I need to tell them that their money isn't actually theirs, but that doesn't sound like a very good business plan. However, I plan to do what God is telling me to do, so I'm just letting you know that if my business craters, you'll know why."

Now, I knew Shawn was a believer. But how was he supposed to react to that news? Our team accounted for about 10% of his branches' revenue. Was I expecting him to high five me? I'm fortunate that he didn't kick me out of his office. He pondered the news, smiled, and said, "Alright, well ... good luck, and keep me posted!"

Whew, I thought afterward. I don't know what I expected, but it felt good to go on record about my new direction.

With the Firm on notice, I went back to the drawing board to try to find the best practices on how to communicate this newfound wisdom of mine. After nearly two years of reading every book and article I could find on the topic, I was stymied. I could not figure out how to change the conversation with clients. Even though the inspiration was always with me, I stuck to my same routine of building and updating plans and investing and monitoring the accounts. Not one thing had changed in my actual behavior—until finally, I had a new inspiration on how to find resources.

One day, as I was bemoaning the fact that I would have to spend the rest of my life coming up with material to communicate biblical wisdom around money, I remembered that one of my father's mentors, Sam Calian, had written a series of articles entitled "The Gospel According to the Wall Street Journal." Sam had worked at Pittsburgh Theological Seminary for 25 years. I decided to dig up Sam's phone number and see if he could help me. When I called him in 2006, he was 72 years old.

Now, this call was totally out of the blue for Sam. When I got him on the phone, however, he didn't act surprised. He patiently listened to me tell the story of my inspiration to communicate differently to clients. When I finished my story, I asked him if those articles he wrote would be a good resource for me or if he knew of any other resources that would be helpful. His answer, delivered in the tone of a compassionate and wise man, was not at all what I expected. He didn't beat around the bush.

"Jeff," he said, "first of all, if God is telling you to do something, I strongly suggest you do it."

That is pretty good advice, I thought.

"Secondly," he continued, "Those articles you mentioned have *nothing* to do with what you are talking about, and I have *no* resources for you."

Rats. My hopes were fading.

"All I know," he finished, "is that you had better be living whatever you are preaching."

There it was.

I felt a lightning bolt of conviction go through my heart when he said that. At that moment, I knew exactly what that meant for me. I had been searching for ways to teach *others* things that I had not fully embraced in *my own life*. I was a hypocrite, and the Holy Spirit convicted me at that moment. In my head and heart, I knew that God owned it all. But, was I acting like it? Were my hands doing enough of what my head and heart knew was right? I knew the answer right then and there. The answer was *no*.

Stunned by this revelation, I awkwardly thanked Sam and hung up. I knew what I needed to do. One of the key things I wanted to communicate with clients was that generosity was important. If God owned it all, and we were supposed to use His money in ways that He would want us to, then we needed to focus on charitable giving as a priority. However, I knew that my family could be more generous. We had been blessed financially, and I felt completely convicted that we needed to give more. Within a few days, I built a new budget for our family that moved giving from the bottom of the budget to the top. The number was much bigger. I took it to Dolly for approval. Truth be told, I harbored a hope that she might talk me down from the cliff. I figured that if she did, well then, I better back off a little since God was certainly into marital harmony.

That talk with Dolly was a turning point. I just assumed that she was more security-minded than me, and that's just how women were wired, right?

Not all women, apparently. Her response to the new giving plan was, "Let's do it!"

"Aren't you worried about running out of money?" I asked.

"No, you'll just make more," she replied.

I didn't know whether to be honored or mortified by her response. *It's not that easy to make money*, I thought to myself, but I did appreciate her confidence in me. The new budget was approved, and we embarked on a new adventure in giving significantly more as a couple.

The Thursday after approving our new budget, I attended a luncheon for The Gathering of Men, a Christian ministry that has groups all over the country. As "luck" would have it, who strolled in and sat down next to me but Peter Forbes, my old Sunday school teacher from when I was in my early twenties. We had kept track of each other off and on, talking only once every few years.

Before the program started, I asked Peter what he was up to. He responded that he was starting something called the Houston Christian Foundation. It sounded like it had to do with the Bible and money.

We didn't have time to talk in detail, as there was a program starting, so I asked him to join me for lunch the following Monday. I spent the entire weekend eagerly awaiting our time together. We met for lunch at Luling City Barbeque. While eating ribs and brisket on butcher paper,

Peter rolled out a presentation titled "The munity Initiative." This initiative included f that were working together. One was Genei organization that held events for high-ca taught them biblical wisdom around generosity, and showed them examples of other families who have gone down that path.

The second non-profit was Crown Financial, an organization that produced small group studies on biblical wisdom around money and possessions. (Howard Dayton, a wonderful mentor of mine and the Founder of Crown, has since started a ministry called Compass that I will discuss later.) The third was the non-profit Peter was helping to start, a local affiliate of the National Christian Foundation (NCF), which was a Christian donor-advised fund that had a niche in helping private business owners make donations of private company stock. Lastly, Peter told me about Kingdom Advisors (KA). This was the icing on the cake. KA, Peter informed me, was a non-profit that educated financial advisors about how to implement biblical wisdom into their practices.

As Peter finished his presentation and looked up from his presentation deck, he must have been surprised to see me staring at him with my jaw nearly on the ground. After two years of trying to figure out how to communicate these principles to clients, I had resigned myself to the fact that I would spend the rest of my life writing, what I gauged to be, 1% of the content that I now realized others had *already* produced. This was a complete answer to prayer. And it was coming from Peter, a source I completely trusted.

Trading Tip #6

The best way to become a change agent is to become a change example. Nothing speaks more powerfully than a changed life. Make sure the changes you are encouraging others to make are ones you are seeking to grow in as well.

Question to Ponder

What primary area in your life needs attention? What one thing can you do each day to help this change occur?

= Physical — eat, drink, exercise, sleep

= available in the moment

7

Changing Management

There are only two kinds of people in the end: those who say to God, "Thy will be done," and those to whom God says, in the end, "Thy will be done."

—C.S. Lewis

I was clearly not in charge of my life. First, God used a seven-year-old to get me deeply involved in Bible study. At that study, He used his Word, my fellow small group participants, teaching, and especially the Holy Spirit to give me an intellectual understanding that He owned everything. He used a fellow believer to guide me to a book by another believer who had felt the same struggle about how to maximize his talents to honor God. After two years of trying to figure out how to communicate this newfound wisdom, God used one of my father's mentors to smack me over the head and teach me that I needed to change my own behavior before I started trying to lead others. Next, God used my wife to teach me about a truly generous attitude. Before the ink was dry on our new family budget, God brought a flood of resources I will never forget. The fact that these resources started flowing within 10 days of our budget change was no coincidence.

There was, however, to be one more test before He allowed me to access those resources.

After Peter finished going down the list of resources available in The Generous Community Initiative, and I was able to wipe the image of him in a Santa Claus suit giving me my entire Christmas list of desires, he asked me a question. He asked if Dolly and I wanted to be "Founders" of this new Houston affiliate of NCF. All I remember saying over and over to him was, "I am all in!" I could not express to him then, or to you now, how big a deal that lunch was to me.

Once again, God had delivered after I showed just a tiny shred of obedience to what He told me to do. I was blown away, thrilled, and reeling. Peter mentioned something about how NCF would collect fees from donor-advised funds (DAF) as operating capital. Dolly and I had a secular DAF, and I told Peter that I would be happy to transfer it to NCF so that his new organization could benefit from the fees it generated.

I was so excited to learn about these new resources, and I wanted to get plugged in immediately, so I had Peter send me the wiring instructions to move over our account immediately. The Thursday after our Monday lunch, I wired all of our secular DAF funds to the NCF account number Peter had provided.

That night, I woke up in a cold sweat at about two in the morning.

I thought, *I don't remember seeing a sub-account number on those wiring instructions.*

And then it hit me. I didn't wire all of the funds to a new sub-account that Dolly and I could still use to give away to other ministries. I had just wired our entire giving budget to the ministry of NCF!

Even though Dolly and I had changed our giving budget on paper, I had not yet moved the new money we budgeted for giving to our DAF before I made that transfer.

My mind spun with what to do.

Should I call Peter first thing in the morning and tell him it was a mistake? Surely, he would understand. It's going to be embarrassing to tell him I know I said I was all in, but I'm not this all in! I thought to myself.

I got out of bed and paced around the house. I fell to my knees and asked God what to do. The response I got was as clear as day. I felt God smiling at me and saying patiently, "Really, Jeff? Is this that tough of a decision? I gave you the wisdom about who is in charge. I gave you the money. I brought you all the resources you've been asking for from a guy you already trust. And now, when you need to give away the extra money that you *already* budgeted but hadn't yet allocated, you are balking?"

I knew right then and there that this was a test. Not a big test by biblical standards, I realize. He wasn't asking me to lead his people out of Egypt like Moses or to slay Goliath like David. No, this test was *custom built* for me. It related to my weak spot—money.

Although I was convinced about what to do, I wanted to get Dolly's approval, too. Even though she had quickly approved the new giving budget, I wasn't exactly sure how she would react to my mistake.

Now, Dolly is not a morning person. So, waking her up at five or six a.m. is generally not a good way to start our day together. However, since I couldn't sleep, as soon as I saw her moving, I woke her up and told her I needed to talk to her. I dragged her down to the dining room table and told her what had happened. I told her I had been up half the night praying about what to do, but that I wanted to check with her first.

When I finished the story, all she said was, "Well, *of course*, you have to leave the money where it is. This opportunity was a total answer to prayer."

And there it was. She didn't have to wrestle with the answer. It was as plain as day. The only one wrestling was me! Schooled again.

I felt at peace that morning when I called Peter to explain what had happened. When he heard the story, he said, "I wondered why our emails didn't make sense."

He was very gracious and offered us the weekend to think and pray about our decision. I remember blurting out, "No! Don't give me the weekend! Cash the check!" I was afraid that if he gave me the extra time that I wouldn't go through with the gift.

Although this is an embarrassing story—I wish I could tell you that I gave the money to NCF voluntarily—it is still a wonderful one for me. Even though God literally had to trick me into giving away all that we budgeted, He was helping me *trade up* in many ways. The first way was that I was *trading up* from a distant walk with Him to an intimate walk with Him. Throughout this experience, I felt God chuckling and rooting for me, like a wonderful, wise grandfather would do. The fact that the Author of the Universe would take the time to personally intervene in my life in such an intimate, tailor-made way was incredible to me. This experience also helped Dolly and me begin the process of *trading up* from a journey of giving out of responsibility to a newfound journey of generosity born out of our thankfulness for what God had done for us.

This surprise gift that God made sure we delivered became our ticket to blessings He had in store for us. While we helped start the Houston NCF affiliate by being founders, we got so much more back from that gift than we gave, as is so often the case. God placed us at the epicenter of what He was doing around generosity in Houston. I was asked to join the Advisory Board of the local NCF affiliate and eventually the Executive Board of that organization, where I served the maximum two terms. Thanks to NCF, I have had the privilege to meet all kinds of wonderful, like-minded believers from all over Houston, who share the same vision of helping inspire Biblical generosity. From the very start, being around those people gave me incredible motivation and inspiration.

At first, I was excited about the services NCF provided that I could use with my clients. What I didn't expect was how much fun it was to be part of a community of Christian leaders from all over the city. Getting to know the stories of the other board members energized me. It was inspiring and comforting to hear that I was not alone. I had neighbors who were actively working out God's plan for their lives. To this day, I am amazed to count many of the people I have met through my involvement there as close friends. I cannot imagine what my life would be like if God hadn't made sure I was part of the NCF family.

While the relationships became the surprise blessing of being involved with NCF, I was also pleased to find the technical resources I was hoping to uncover. One of the key things I learned was that NCF had a cadre of lawyers on staff that worked on more "illiquid gifts" than any other ministry or DAF. These illiquid gifts were often appreciated private company stock or real estate. Before finding NCF, I had never heard of such a thing. This tool became a tremendous arrow in our team's quiver for the generous business owners God brought our way. Our team has had the blessing of working with many families who have used NCF's team to facilitate the donation of substantial resources to their God-given passions. It makes our clients' giving simpler. Each year we transfer appreciated shares of stock to our clients' account DAFs, which has the double advantages of avoiding capital gains tax on the appreciated stock and centralizing our clients' record-keeping. Having one account to receive and distribute their charitable gifts makes their lives easier. In recent years, we have also discovered other wonderful Christian DAFs, including Water-Stone and The Signatry.

I went all-in with the other ministries of the Generous Community Initiative as well. I trained to become a small group leader for Crown Ministries. Crown's mission at the time was to produce small group Bible studies that centered on discovering God's wisdom around money and possessions. I joined a small group Crown study, made up of various people I had met through NCF, called the "Special Edition." The Special Edition focused on content specific to those who had more than they needed, which was especially relevant for the world I worked in every day. Even though most of the families my team helped would not describe themselves as "rich" (they reserved that word for those who had even more than they did), they actually were very rich by the world's standards. According to Credit

Suisse's 2018 Global Wealth Report, it only takes about $700k in net assets to be in the top one percent globally.

Crown's study helped me process better questions to ask to get a more meaningful conversation going. I attended all kinds of events that Crown put on for their volunteers in the community. At one point, I had the pleasure of meeting the founder, Howard Dayton, who proved to be an incredibly engaged, energetic, and humble guy. What I think impressed me the most, however, was how *happy* he was. This guy went around the world, teaching generosity and frugality, and he was full of joy. His enthusiasm was infectious, and I was a sponge for it. He has since started a new ministry called Compass, whose vision is to teach people worldwide how to handle money and operate businesses God's way. Howard has become an important mentor in my life. He continues to be incredibly generous to me with his time and wisdom and models how to live a godly life.

Generous Giving was another one of the non-profits in the Generous Community Initiative. Fully funded by the Maclellan Foundation, they never ask for money. That fact is amazing in and of itself. However, what is more impressive is the work they do in helping people learn more about biblical generosity. They put on events all over the country that have content rotating between biblical teaching and testimonies from other people who have experienced the joy of giving. The first Generous Giving conference Dolly and I attended was in Chicago in 2007, the same year we became Founders of the NCF affiliate in Houston.

I'll never forget one of the testimonies I heard at that event. A regal 60-year-old woman stood at the podium and told the story of how she and her husband were empty nesters and had agreed to host two Russian exchange students. These high-school-age girls wanted to spend the summer in the U.S. to see what this American dream was all about. The speaker felt apprehensive at the thought of entertaining teenagers, something she hadn't done in a while. So, she decided that she would just take them wherever she went. After all, she was living the American dream these girls came to see. She would give them a front-row seat.

This woman and her husband had been very successful financially. They had a big home in the suburbs, a brownstone they were remodeling in the city of Chicago, and they were building their dream lake house outside of town. The speaker spent the entire summer taking these girls from one house to the other. At the end of the summer, she asked the girls what they thought of her lifestyle. She thought they would express their awe at the luxurious life they lived. Instead, the girls said, "We are exhausted. We are worn out from running around, helping you take care of your stuff! We can't wait to get back to our little apartment in Russia!"

While there was incredible biblical teaching at the conference, this story was what stuck with me, and I have used it often with clients when I needed a helpful illustration. This story prompted me to think about how much stuff we had accumulated and how too often it felt like our stuff owned us. I found the words in the old hymn, "There Is No Gain But by a Loss," quite relatable:

> Our souls are held by all they hold;
> slaves still are slaves in chains of gold.[1]

The last of the Generous Community Initiative nonprofits was Kingdom Advisors. The mission of Kingdom Advisors was to encourage and equip advisors to integrate biblical wisdom into their advice, which lined up perfectly with my personal game plan. That this organization even existed amazed me!

When God gave me the game plan to implement biblical wisdom into my financial advisory practice, I thought I would have to spend the rest of my life inventing ways to communicate His wisdom. It was as if God told me to build a sailboat. Trying to be obedient, I downloaded some fuzzy plans for a small Sunfish-style sailboat from the internet. As I stepped back from my work, I noticed the mast was crooked; this thing was unlikely to sail straight any time soon. Then, thankfully, God sent Peter Forbes to me in an America's Cup racing sailboat with big sails, a huge hull made of the latest Nasa-inspired materials, and an experienced crew. Peter stood on the deck of the boat looking down at me, smiling, and said, "Why don't you get up here with us, young man? I think you'll go a lot faster." I couldn't wait to jump on the Kingdom Advisors' boat and put on the team sweater!

The Kingdom Advisors' roots were planted in 1997 when Larry Burkett, co-founder of Crown Financial Ministries, brought together 16 close friends and fellow professionals with a commitment to incorporating biblical wisdom into their advice and counsel and formed the Christian Financial Planning Institute (CFPI).

In 2003, they set forth on a mission to advance this vision by creating a new organization that would take the lead in reaching out to the Christian financial professional community. Originally known as the Christian Financial

Professionals Network (CFPN) under the leadership of Ron Blue, the organization began to grow and thrive over the next four years and, in 2007, was renamed Kingdom Advisors (KA).

Thanks to Peter, I found KA soon after its formation in 2007. I joined a monthly study group for KA members from all over Houston. From that group, I learned that there was a Qualified KA training program (now called the Certified Kingdom Advisor designation) available online. I signed up as soon as I could. The training contained 20 modules where you would watch a video about a biblical principle that related to money and then would work through a workbook and formulate your convictions about that principle. Using the material as my quiet time in the morning, I finished it in a few weeks. Much later, I found out that I was the third Qualified KA in Houston. The only two other people who had the designation were employees of Ronald Blue & Co., a boutique Christian financial planning firm that KA founder, Ron Blue, had started nearly 30 years prior.

During that training, I had a couple of "Ah-ha!" moments. At one point, Ron prompted the viewer to think about their unique position, not just with clients, but with co-workers. The challenge was to think about what kind of example you were setting in the office. That challenge woke me up! I had always prided myself on keeping my head down and doing my work. In the financial advisory business, there is a high failure rate, and I had witnessed a lot of complaining from failing advisors about how their failure was someone else's fault. They generally directed that blame at firm management in one way or another. Being a singles tennis player, I was more than happy to take on the burden of success or failure for myself. However, this solitary focus on my own path didn't leave much room for social interaction around the office. I generally had my head down as I moved quickly around the office without much acknowledgment of others. It was like I was operating a snowplow, cutting a narrow path in the drifts. I just wanted to clear my walk and keep moving.

For most of my career, I worked in an office that posted a printed daily reminder of how much production (revenue) each advisor in the office produced. When I started in the industry, of course, I was near the bottom of the list. However, now that I was near the top of the leaderboard, I was still acting like I was at the bottom. Hearing Ron's challenge to consider what others in the office were learning from my behavior convicted me. As I reflected on his comments, I realized that even when I was on the bottom of the production rung, I always kept my eye on the leaders.

I would ask myself, "How did they behave?" I took cues from them. Those cues came from the way I saw them interact with their clients, their teams, management, and me. For the first time, I grasped that I was now one of the top producers being watched.

Uh-oh, I thought. *How have I been behaving?*

It gave me an all-new awareness and feeling of responsibility toward those around me who weren't directly involved in my business. I consciously slowed down to show more interest in the person next to me at the coffee pot or the printer. It was fun to get to know them and provide them with a little encouragement.

Around the time of this revelation, I remember chatting with a new advisor in the hallway near the printer. As I headed back to my office, one of the older advisors in the office stopped me in the hallway. He asked, "Why are you talking to these new advisors?"

I didn't quite know what to say. I think I mumbled something like, "He's a nice guy."

The old advisor turned to me and said, "I never introduce myself to anyone who hasn't been around for at least three years. So few of these new folks make it that it's a waste of time to talk to them before then."

One of the other lessons I learned from the Qualified KA training was from a story about the owners of the Chris Craft boat company. Prior to World War II, the owners had started their company and had great success. Toward the end of the war, they got a huge order from the U.S. military. They were thrilled. They went to the bank and took out a huge loan to fulfill the order only to find out shortly after the ink dried on the loan documents that the war was winding down and the order had been canceled. The expense of ramping up to fulfill that order and taking on debt sank (pardon the pun) the company. They declared bankruptcy, and the judge erased their debt obligations. At that point in the story, I figured this was a tale warning of the risks of too much debt—but that wasn't the only point being made.

The owners of the company painfully, but successfully, revived the company post-bankruptcy. The amazing thing was that even though the courts extinguished their debts, they spent decades painstakingly tracking every vendor and lender they owed money to and paying them back. Can you imagine the surprise on the faces of some of these vendors who got checks for debts they had long-since written off? Talk about countercultural!

Stories like these began piling up for me. They were extraordinary examples of faithful people acting in extraordinary ways to be a blessing to those around them. They were concrete illustrations of the famous quote by St. Francis Assisi: "Preach the gospel at all times. If necessary, use words."

Not long after I completed the Qualified KA training, I sent a letter addressed to Ron Blue and KA management, telling them how thankful I was for the material they had compiled. It was truly an amazing experience to soak up wisdom in a matter of months that I thought would take decades to learn.

Over the next couple of years, I got to know the leadership of KA. I was part of a group of advisors that invited to their headquarters in Atlanta periodically to help with the strategic direction of the organization. It was a thrill for me to get to know the hearts of KA management and fellow advisors from various firms around the country who had similar interests. I was very impressed with the quality of leadership talent KA had recruited inside their organization and from the advisor community.

In 2009, I got a call from Rob West, now the president of KA, asking if I would be interested in being a "coach" for the new KA Coaching Program they were starting. About 50 KA members from all over the country signed up to fly to Atlanta once a quarter for three years and attend 24 hours of training. Rob asked me if I would be willing to coach a table of advisors from large brokerage firms, and I agreed. Truthfully, at that time, I was more of a "player" than a "coach." But that was all about to change.

Trading Tip #7

Trade present understanding for ongoing curiosity. We can never become too knowledgeable about our craft, but we can easily become stale and cynical, especially as we get older. People who do something extraordinary with their lives and jobs never rest on the laurels of past learning or achievements.

Question to Ponder

Who or what are the best learning venues in your life? Who are you not fully taking advantage of that would be most helpful?

---

[1] Arthur Sydney Booth-Clibborn, "There Is No Gain but By a Loss," hymnal.net, accessed October 3, 2019, https://www.hymnal.net/en/hymn/h/623?type=a&loop=2&delay=0.

WSJ / BIBLE

PEOPLE w/ EXPERTISE (w/ GOOD WORLDVIEW)

8

Developing a New Strategy

*Life in time remains without meaning if it does not
find its meaning in eternity.*

—N. A. Berdyaev

I truly enjoyed being a part of the Kingdom Advisors' Coaching
Program from 2009 to 2011. Once a quarter, I flew to Atlanta
from Houston with about 50 other advisors from around
the country from various firms, large and small. I wanted
to learn directly from Ron Blue and the team he assembled.
Several key teachings helped me build a foundation for the
way I would communicate to clients and other advisors.

Lloyd Reeb of Halftime led a few of the sessions. I
wrote about Halftime earlier. Their mission is to help people of all walks of life move from success to significance.
Lloyd essentially led us through the content of the Halftime
Institute, the primary coaching program of that organization. Since Bob Buford was Halftime's founder, the process
I learned in those sessions was an expanded version of
what I learned in his books. One of my favorite parts of

those sessions was the story Lloyd told about one of the Institute graduates named Kenneth Yeung. Here's the story, as Lloyd tells it in his book, *The Second Half*:

> Kenneth Yeung introduced himself to a small group of Asian-American business leaders by saying, "I'm Kenneth, I'm 57, and I am a tea guy. I am married and we have one daughter, and I am passionate about orphans."
>
> I was intrigued. I wanted to know what he meant by "a tea guy" and what he did for orphans. As the day progressed, I explored what he meant and how those two things had shaped his past, while he learned how they would shape his future. Kenneth had a secret assumption when he arrived at the beautiful hotel part way up the mountain in Vail, Colo. I was leading the small group of peers on a day-long exploration of "what to do with the second half of life." He assumed he was destined to someday sell his company, go to seminary, and become a minister. What he discovered was something radically different, but not at all radically different from who Kenneth is at the core. A picture can indeed speak a thousand words, but for Kenneth, it was the words on a poster featuring the photo of a young Chinese girl that spoke to his very soul: "Priority – A hundred years from now it will not matter what my bank account was, the sort of house I lived in, or the kind of car I drove. But the world may be different because I was important in the life of a child."

A native of the Shantou, Guang Dong province of China; Kenneth understands more than most the meaning behind that message. Political oppression forced his mother to send him to live with relatives in Hong Kong, where he struggled with language and cultural differences, as well as heart-wrenching homesickness. What 11-year-old wouldn't? But sensing the hole in his heart and the voids in his life skills, caring neighbors reached out to boost him over the language hurdle and to bridge the gap of his parent less world. "I learned early on in life that it is so important for someone to give you a helping hand if you don't have help from a family member," says Kenneth.

Several years later, an equally caring teacher started Kenneth on a spiritual journey. As he matured in his faith, one thing was certain: He wanted to help others as his way of giving back. He prayerfully contemplated a career in ministry or social work. "But God had higher plans for my life," he says. "He led me to San Francisco, not into social work, but into business – and He expanded my influence far beyond what I could have ever imagined."

That business—a highly successful tea company—operates with an unwritten contract with God. "When I started the business," he says, "I told my Lord that I wanted to serve Him. 'This is your business. I am just your steward to manage it for you.' That unwritten contract guides how I treat my employees – and how I use the funds the business generates."

The substantial profits his company generates are invested in meeting the deepest needs of others, Kenneth says, not his own comfort or material gain. He first began by using profits to help hundreds of American families adopt Chinese children when no agency in America knew how to go about it. In 1993, Kenneth and his wife also adopted a Chinese baby, Melissa Joy, who every day of her life puts her fingerprints on the message of the poster that had so captivated her father's heart.

When I asked Kenneth about what he does with orphans, his eyes lit up and he simply said, "Would you like to see my photos? We built an orphanage in China." He reached down and pulled out a dog-eared little photo album and began to show me the most compelling shots of an orphanage for 100 little children, all of them disabled. Page 7 was a photo of him holding a little girl, and I was captivated by the smile on his face. "Who is this little girl," I asked, "and why are you smiling like that?" He told me her name and said, "I just paid to have her heart repaired. Without that, she would have been disposable."

Now that took my breath away. In China, where baby girls are often abandoned, the opportunity to make a difference in the life of a child is great—so great that in 1995 Kenneth began an endeavor that took eight years to bring to fruition. Considered an embarrassment to their families, the mentally and physically handicapped of China often are thrown into garbage bins. Burdened to make a home for these unwanted children, Kenneth negotiated patiently with the Chinese government. In November 2003, the Prince of Peace Children's Home (POPCH), located in the Wuqing district of Tianjin, opened its doors. Funded by the Prince of Peace Foundation and World Vision International as a joint venture with the Civil Affairs Bureau of Wuqing, the facility accommodates 100 mentally and physically handicapped children under age 6 and provides rehabilitation services to other disabled children in the province. The home set a miraculous precedent in China: For the first time in history; the government had allowed a foreign organization to build, staff, and manage an orphanage. Today, highly trained staff and caring volunteers lovingly embrace children once viewed as society's trash—and they teach others to do the same.

"I told the Chinese officials that we would not only build and manage the orphanage, but we would also set up a training center to help caretakers from other orphanages in China," Kenneth says. "What the Chinese government really needs is to see a model that an overseas Christian organization can come in and build this type of thing with love and care. I told the officials that God has loved us, and we want to share our love with the children in China. They accepted that. They even allowed us to engrave a Bible verse on the cornerstone of the building."

At lunch during our time in Colorado, I asked Kenneth if he left any other passions behind during his first-half pursuit of success. After just a few seconds he looked me straight in the eyes and said, "Well, yes, there is. I am very good at photography. I love photography, but about 15 years ago I gave it up because my business was growing and my family was busy." The biggest thrill for me at the end of that day was to sit back and listen as Kenneth shared with his peers a plan for his second half of life. "I came to this day thinking I would sell my business and go to seminary and go into ministry," he said, "But I'm a tea guy—this is what I do and I am good at it and I make a lot of money doing it. So instead, I am going to hire someone to take some of my responsibilities in my company, and I will go and capture the most compelling photos of disabled orphans in China to challenge others to help fund orphanages for these children—we'll even print them on the back of the tea packages we sell around the world. And I will go and ensure they are run well."

And that is exactly what he is doing. In fact, these are his photographs and they represent the convergence of his passions: Tea company profits, compelling photographs and disabled orphans who know every day that someone loves them dearly. He recently won a prestigious award by the Chinese government for outstanding charitable organizations—the first non-Chinese citizen to receive the award. Kenneth put it this way: "If I can help change the fate of a needy child, I'd rather do that than have all the world's luxury."

What caught my attention about this story was that Ken was a business guy who felt called to help orphans. It seemed that Ken, like myself, felt that if you were "called to ministry," then you had to walk away from your for-profit business. People who were "called to ministry" only work for non-profits, right? The paradigm shift of titanic proportions continued working its magic into my soul. Perhaps being called to ministry wasn't about walking away from one's secular job in order to serve God more fully. I was beginning to see what the Bible has said all along: full-time ministry is doing the best with what God has entrusted us so that His name and His love penetrates the cracks and crevices of where the vast majority of people spend most of their time—the working world. The first 300 years of Christianity were spent doing exactly this. And this was a huge reason they had such success in spreading the Gospel.

As he was struggling with this decision, Ken enrolled in the Halftime Institute. It was there that he did the same assignment that Lloyd Reeb led our KA Coaching Class through. We spent time listing out the skills and experiences God had given each one of us and considered how we might maximize those things for a higher purpose going forward, how we could *trade up*, in other words, from just living life to living a life of purpose. We also spent time with a small group of others discussing our thoughts.

In Ken's case, his game plan changed as he discussed his passions and skills with others in his group. The group helped Ken come up with a new plan by identifying that he was a talented businessman with a passion for orphans and photography. They determined that if he completely abandoned the business, he would not be leveraging all of his gifts. So, collectively, they came up with the idea that Ken would continue to own and supervise the tea company but hire a manager for the business. He would then be free to engage his photography talents and place one of his photographs on the back of every package of tea with a website address below it, directing consumers to consider joining him in his mission of caring for orphans. Ken was excited by the new plan to combine his experience and skills more cohesively. He was able to have an increased impact on his true calling—helping orphans. This new plan brought in far more funding for the orphans than the sale of the business would have done.

I love that story and have told it innumerable times because it proves that a person's maximum impact does not depend on the tax status of his employer. It proves that the key to self-actualizing is to find a God-honoring, others-centered mission that you are passionate about, and then align your talents and experience to maximize your impact in that area. It is the difference between a rainbow and a laser. The rainbow is beautiful and is caused by a refraction of light in many different directions. A laser focuses light in one direction and puts off a lot more heat!

One of the other things I love about Ken's story is that it took a team to come up with the best plan for his life. It was yet another lesson to me that *life is a team sport*, not a singles tennis match!

At the KA Coaching sessions led by Lloyd of Halftime, we went through the same process of allowing others to help us craft our personal mission statement. Mine came to be, "I will use my financial services platform to pour into the lives of high-capacity families to help them uncover their God-given calling and give them oxygen to live it out." I could think of nothing more exciting than spending the rest of my career helping people like Ken refine their calling!

Two of my other favorite teachings at the KA Coaching Program came from Jim Wise. One of Jim's teachings was called "The Skilled Craftsman." He told the story of Moses going to the top of Mount Sinai to commune with God while the Israelites were in the desert. After his extended absence, the people started to grumble and complain that they were better off as slaves in Egypt. To remind them of "those good ol' days," the people ordered the skilled craftsmen of their day to melt down their gold jewelry and turn it into a golden calf that they would worship like the Egyptians. You can imagine Moses' reaction when he returned to their midst. He was not pleased! He made the people melt down the idol and drink it. Yet, in later chapters, the craftsman of Israel used those same talents for the God-honoring job of building the ark of the covenant.

Jim did a brilliant job of simply asking us a few questions: aren't financial advisors "skilled craftsmen" of the financial industry? If so, are we helping make idols or helping in godly endeavors? What constituted "making idols" in our business? What constituted a godly endeavor?

These questions hit me hard and clarified my task ahead. It gave me a framework for how to think about the meaning of my work. As discussed in earlier chapters, I knew there were things I needed to change in the way I delivered financial advice. What came next, in my other favorite teachings from Jim, were practical tools to help me do just that.

These teachings centered around the practical concept of meeting clients and prospects where they were spiritually. What most helped me was the suggestion that when we meet folks, we should ask enough questions and pick up on enough clues to try to visualize them on a "spiritual spectrum" — from 1 (hostile to God) to 10 (super tight with God).

Jim told a great story about being invited by a prospect to her home. Upon arriving, he couldn't help noticing that she had small idols all around the house. Jim asked us to think about how we would react. Trying to imagine myself in that situation, I thought that my initial reaction would be, "Get me out of here!" Jim's reaction was much different. While looking at the idols, he said, "I can see that you are a very spiritual person. So am I."

I loved his response and learned a lot from it. I needed to stop making snap judgments about people, build bridges, and see them for their potential.

Jim's story reminded me of a talk that my good friend Dwight Edwards once gave about the concept of potential. Dwight is a pastor and speaker with a heart for helping business people wake up to their ministry potential in the business world. Dwight's story focused on Michaelangelo's work on the famous statue *David* from 1501 to 1504. In 1464, a Florentine sculptor named Agostino di Duccio was contracted to produce a sculpture of *David*. A large block of marble was brought from a quarry in Northern Tuscany for him to work on. He worked for a few years and then gave up on the project. Ten years later, another sculptor named Antonio Rossellino picked up the work where di Duccio left off. But he too gave up on the project after his contract ran out. For 25 years, the block of marble lay exposed to all the elements of nature. Then Michelangelo came along.

He took that exact piece of marble and fashioned it into one of the greatest works of art known to man. You can see it today in the Academia Gallery, in Florence, Italy. When asked where he got the inspiration for the work, he replied, "I saw the angel in the marble and carved until I set him free." Elsewhere Michelangelo writes,

> In every block of marble I see a statue as plain as though it stood before me, shaped and perfect in attitude and action. I have only to hew away the rough walls that imprison the lovely apparition to reveal it to the other eyes as mine see it.

What I loved about that story was that it gave me a vision for how God sees us. He doesn't see us as the hopeless, big block of unrefined marble as many others do. He sees us as a masterpiece in progress. That's how I wanted to look at myself, my team, and our clients—as masterpieces in progress!

Jim's talk of meeting people where they are and encouraging them also reminded me of a great talk on encouragement that I had heard from John Collier years earlier. John was an associate pastor at West University United Methodist Church, where I had the privilege of getting to know him. After retiring from the Church, he started a ministry called Caring Friends, Inc. He still uses that platform to encourage and serve people all over the city of Houston and beyond. I've made him tell me this story multiple times. It is about the difference an unexpected encourager made in his life at the age of 14 in 1957.

John grew up in the small town of Lufkin, Texas. When he was 14 years old, he had just made the local all-star baseball team. After one game, it was raining, and the parking lot was rutted and full of puddles. His teammate and friend, Cue Boykin, and Cue's father, C.D. Boykin, were walking with him to the car. On that walk, C.D. turned to John and said, "John, you could be the best 14-year-old pitcher in the state of Texas."

Upon hearing this bold statement, a dazed John Collier stepped directly in a puddle. John was reeling from the idea that this could possibly be true. He wasn't even sure if he was the best pitcher on his all-star team, let alone the entire state of Texas! John rushed home and told his dad what Mr. Boykin had said. His dad backed up Mr. Boykin's statement and added, "You should ask Mr. Boykin what you can do to make that outcome more likely."

So, John did. Mr. Boykin replied, "I'm glad you asked! You should work on being great at two curveballs instead of being decent at five curveballs."

John took his advice, and the results were amazing. He credits Mr. Boykin with giving him a vision far beyond what he had ever considered for himself. John Collier ended up having incredible success in baseball throughout high school and in college at the University of Texas. He had a chance to play professionally but turned it down in favor of attending seminary. When John tells this story, it is as if it happened to him yesterday—and it was 62 years ago as I write this!

Every time I hear these stories, I am inspired by the power of encouragement. **Life is a team sport**. We need others to lift us up, to help us see our God-given potential, and to spur us on. Often this involves narrowing our focus to the few "pitches" that we are great at throwing.

Nothing gives me more pleasure than encouraging people in this way. My primary delivery system is the financial services business. Financially-successful people have to seek advice somewhere. When they cross my path, I want to steward that relationship well and help them raise their sights on what is possible.

After the first year of the KA Coaching Program, I was ecstatic about what I was learning. However, I felt that I could still benefit from a mentor. I finally got up the courage at one of the KA Coaching Program breaks to ask KA Founder, Ron Blue, if he would spend some time with me one-on-one in the mornings before we started our first sessions. Ron graciously agreed, and during the final two years of the program, we would get together in the restaurant of the Atlanta Airport Hilton and talk. There are two specific stories Ron told me that will forever stick with me and inspired me on my path.

He told the first story, the story of Nehemiah, when I asked him about his vision for the financial services industry. He explained that Nehemiah worked for a foreign king but became very concerned about his people, the Israelites. He finally got up the courage to ask his boss if he could take some time off (he was a slave, so vacation wasn't really in his contract) to go and help his people. Fortunately, his master, King Artaxerxes, let him go and even equipped him for his mission. Nehemiah's goal was to rebuild the walls around Jerusalem. When he got to Jerusalem, he enlisted all of the various tribes to claim a section of the wall that they would be responsible for rebuilding.

Ron used this story to illustrate how his vision for Kingdom Advisors was to lead the rebuilding of Wall Street the way Nehemiah led the rebuilding of the walls of Jerusalem. Ron said that on the topic of money, Main Street listens to Wall Street. So, if we could change the way Wall Street dispensed wisdom, we could change the way America thought about money.

Wow, I thought. *That is a huge goal. I want to be part of it.*

The second story from Ron that influenced my vision was when told me that he was good at starting things, but, he chuckled, "they always got bigger and better after I left." He used the example of Ronald Blue & Co., a financial planning firm he had started from scratch over 30 years prior that grew rapidly after he left it. He told me that he couldn't believe that, at the time we spoke, it had grown to 15 offices doing $50mm in revenue.

Ron was the classic visionary. He proved there was an appetite for biblical wisdom in finance. He and Howard Dayton had stood on the shoulders of Larry Burkett. Now Dave Ramsey and people like me were standing on Howard's and Ron's shoulders, rebuilding our part of Wall Street, claiming territory for Christ. Rarely is the early mover the one that scales the idea.

When Ron shared this story with me, I felt God saying to me, "I want you to scale what Ron started." Although it wasn't audible, it was the clearest I've ever heard God speak to me. I looked over both shoulders to see if there was someone behind me that could actually pull that off!

Instantly, I began processing what this meant. It sounded like fun! I had spent my entire career in scaled environments. I knew how they operated. At that point, the office I was working in at Morgan Stanley was doing $50mm in revenue, and there were eight such offices in Houston alone. Fifty million dollars in revenue was not even on the radar nationally. My mind was racing 100 miles per hour. I had many opinions on how large firms could operate more effectively. I had shared my opinions with management in all kinds of different forums, including on the Advisory Board for the Morgan Stanley Bank that had been established after the financial crisis of 2008-2009.

Then the doubts started to creep in. While I had operated a large team within a scaled environment, I had never scaled *anything*.

I'm unqualified, I thought.

I felt God immediately respond, "I equip the called; I don't call the equipped."

I knew in a nanosecond that if I ever had a shred of success scaling something, I would give all the credit to God — because He was going to have to guide me every step of the way.

While it was overwhelmingly exciting to have such a clear vision literally put in my lap, it was also daunting. When God gives you a vision, he doesn't tell you all the steps to achieve it right then and there. He gives you a vision ending at "Z," and you are at "A." He gives us the challenge and the joy of waking up every day and asking Him, "What do I do next?"

Trading Tip #8

Exchange seeing people in light of their problems for seeing them in light of their potential. Learn to focus on the angel in every person you meet more than their marble. People respond most powerfully to hope and encouragement. Become a specialist in those two commodities.

Question to Ponder

Who is the person you are most tempted to write off? Look deeper and see if you can find the hidden potential which is awaiting release.

9

The Path Forward

*So many people live within unhappy circumstances
and yet will not take the initiative to change their
situation because they are conditioned to a life of
security, conformity, and conservation, all of which
appear to give one peace of mind, but in reality,
nothing is more damaging to the adventurous spirit.*

—Christopher McCandless

When God gives you a vision, He doesn't tell you every step it will take to achieve that vision, which is a good thing. We probably wouldn't take the first step if we knew what all would be involved! Also, if we knew all the steps from start to finish, then we wouldn't have to stay connected and dependent on God every step of the way. It would rob us of the adventure!

It was 2010 when God gave me the vision to scale what Ron started. Since I still had some risk-averse accountant in me, I figured the best place to start was where I was planted. When God got ahold of me in 2007, I feared that the business would collapse because I was going to start telling everyone their money wasn't really theirs. However,

God did the opposite—He blessed my business. For the first time in my career, in 2008, I made the Chairman's Club (top 2%) of advisors at Morgan Stanley. This put me in the top 1% of advisors nationwide. From 2009-2013, I was recognized by Barron's magazine as "One of Texas' Top Financial Advisors." In 2013, the Financial Times named me to their inaugural list of "America's Top 400 Advisors." My production climbed from $1mm in 2000 to well over $2mm by the time I left Morgan Stanley in 2017. None of this happened before I turned my life and business completely over to Christ.

But I'm getting ahead of myself in telling the story!

I first tried to fulfill the vision God gave me at Morgan Stanley. I wanted to leverage any favor I had at the Firm into building a group of like-minded advisors inside the company.

In 2007, I had started the Christian Focus Group at Morgan Stanley. During some of the Kingdom Advisors strategic planning sessions in Atlanta, I formed a friendship with a guy named Jeff Cave from Merrill Lynch. At that time, he was working in the New York corporate office of Merrill. While he didn't have a book of his own, he helped advisors close institutional business. He shared a vision for the importance of biblical wisdom in finance and started something called the Christian Focus Group at Merrill Lynch.

Although the Group was not formally recognized, Jeff and his leadership team had come up with a winsome way of communicating the purpose of the Group to Merrill management. It was a niche marketing group focused on the Christian marketplace. Regardless of advisors' personal beliefs, they could join the Group and learn how the Christian marketplace thought about money—as stewards instead of owners. This approach allowed Jeff and his team of volunteer leaders to cobble together an email list of several hundred members.

I thought this was a fantastic idea! Fortunately, Jeff was very generous with his time and advice in helping me set up the same thing at Morgan Stanley. By 2010, when God gave me the vision for scale, we had a decent email list of advisors that were interested in the topic. I would regularly host conference calls to encourage advisors who were serving the Christian marketplace.

My first idea for scale was to build the Christian Focus Group at Morgan Stanley and develop a sub-section of the Group as a "SWAT team" of like-minded advisors to help them implement biblical wisdom into their practices. I was hoping that perhaps over time, the Group and this SWAT team could influence the culture of Wall Street from within one of its' biggest players.

By 2014, we had about 160 names on the Christian Focus Group email list. We had a small band of volunteer leaders that would spread the word about the Group and help lead conference calls when I wasn't available. My primary partner in helping lead the Group was Brad Hulse out of Indianapolis. We met at the Kingdom Advisors Coaching Program years before, and he helped me lead and ultimately grow the Group.

For years, Brad and I tried to get Morgan Stanley management to officially recognize the Group in some way. I like to describe the period from 2007 to 2014 as "mid-level lawyer purgatory." Finally, in 2014, the logjam broke thanks to another member's efforts. Phil Shaffer was one of the founders of an institutional consulting group called Graystone. Graystone had been a part of Smith Barney and was acquired when Morgan Stanley purchased Smith Barney in 2009. In 2014, the legacy Smith Barney people were forced onto Morgan Stanley's computer platform, and it was messy. Members of the Graystone group had a contentious meeting with Morgan Stanley management, and Phil had helped quell the rebellion. He called me right afterward and said he had a chip to play with management and wanted to play it on getting the Christian Focus Group approved. Long story short, Phil following through, and the Group got approved in the form of a web page on the internal intranet of Morgan Stanley!

We had one more ask of management, in addition to the website, which was to send an email to everyone in the Firm's wealth management unit announcing the Group's existence. While management wasn't willing to do that, they did agree to write an article on the success of someone in the Group serving the Christian marketplace and include a link to join the Christian Focus Group. The leadership team of the Group suggested they write the article on my team. So, Morgan Stanley hired a local Houston photographer to take pictures of our team as well as a writer from Los Angeles to draft the story. It was published in an electronic periodical that highlighted multiple success stories from around the Firm.

Within a few days of the article's publication, we increased membership from 160 to 450. By the time our team left to start our own company in 2017, the Group had nearly 600 members.

That period of rapid growth for the Christian Focus Group was an exciting time. I started to get phone calls and emails nearly every day from someone in the Group asking, "How do I build a God-honoring business at this firm?"

Every time I got one of those calls or emails, I wound up spending the next 90 minutes telling them the story in this book. In fact, that's a big reason I started writing this book—so I could send it to them and tell them to call me back if they were still interested in talking!

At any rate, our team was functioning well and growing. Pat Combs joined our team in 2009. He was still living in Dallas and was completely aligned with the vision and mission we were pursuing. Our team grew and partnered with nearly 50 advisors around the Firm at one point or another.

By 2016, however, it became clear that we weren't going to be able to achieve the vision God had given us at Morgan Stanley.

Many signs made this obvious—from the rulings of the legal department on various topics, including restrictions on communications involving Bible verses, to platform limitations on how we could effectively partner with other advisors. I could write an entire book on this topic, but suffice it to say that after 17 years at Morgan Stanley, I knew it was time to leave. I mourned the death of achieving our God-given vision at Morgan Stanley. After all, I had many friends there and golden handcuffs that were gleaming and strong. However, God had already dealt with me on the money topic, so I trusted He would show us the path forward.

Fortunately, He did. God began showing me a new path for our part in rebuilding Wall Street—the path of an independent firm. After researching and praying about every conceivable option, I felt peace about this new path forward.

So, in April of 2017, we launched Archetype Wealth Partners. Our big, holy, audacious goal was, and still is, to ultimately become one of the country's top 20 wealth management companies. We want to be the "Chick-Fil-A of wealth management." While they don't stamp the cross into their chicken sandwiches, the owners of the company are unapologetically Christian, and they run the business using Christian principles. Oh, and their stores are nearly twice as productive as the average McDonalds. If they can do it in fast food, why can't we do it in the wealth management business?

We are building a private company that will never change its' vision or mission. We are intentionally avoiding debt and private equity investment to ensure we avoid the pressure to do so. Over the course of my career, I've seen what those pressures can do. They often lead to transactions that ruin the culture. We think it is critical to start with the end in mind—a company of aligned employees that provides complete representation to clients on a purely fiduciary platform. Archetype means "ideal model." Our vision is "to build the ideal, God-honoring wealth management company." Our mission is "to help families thrive across generations by connecting their money to their purpose."

When we launched the company, we went on a listening tour to learn from other like-minded business owners and executives. One of our first stops was to visit Ron Blue himself, as well as other former leaders in his organization. Ron told us that he never intended to scale his wealth management business. He encouraged us to use a different structure more suited for scale. We also visited with Chick-Fil-A and Hobby Lobby management. Those organizations had learned many lessons on their way to scale, and they were incredibly valuable. We are grateful to be standing on the shoulders of these amazing leaders.

God revealed a path that would let us take advantage of several large industry trends, along with the freedom to communicate His principles in a God-honoring way. As Wayne Gretzky would say, we started "skating to where the puck was going to be" in the industry.

The primary decision we made was to offer clients what we now call "*Complete Representation*." This term has many facets to it. One of them is our *legal position* in relation to the client. Our firm is solely registered with the SEC as a "Registered Investment Advisor" (RIA). This is legal jargon that means our Firm represents the client 100% of the time. At the biggest national firms like Morgan Stanley and Merrill Lynch, the advisor wears many legal hats. Those hats often change (unbeknownst to the client) during one fluid conversation. When talking with a client about mortgages at those firms, the advisor represents the bank, not the client. When talking about insurance, the advisor represents the insurance company, not the client. When talking about buying a commissionable mutual fund, the advisor represents the brokerage firm, not the client. In certain situations, the advisor can represent the client if he or she offers a particular product, but it is all very confusing to the client or prospect. As an RIA-only firm, we represent clients 100% of the time, so that there is no confusion. Industry statistics show that RIA-only firms are rapidly gaining market share.

A second important facet of Complete Representation was to incorporate a *broader range of service offerings* to clients. We call our services "The Four Quadrants." We offer

3x the services that a typical advisor at our old Firm offers. The reason the service offerings are so limited is that, at the big firms, the brokerage divisions were founded by investment banks over a hundred years ago. Back then, the brokers' job was to sell the stocks and bonds of companies, like the railroads, to finance their expansion.

Unfortunately, the industry hasn't evolved much since then. A vast majority of advisors still only focus on selling one product—investments. While we think investments are important and our Investment Committee spends a lot of time on our investment approach, it is just one of The Four Quadrants.

The second of The Four Quadrants service offerings is what we call "Strategy." Before we left Morgan Stanley, I remember management quoting a statistic that only 6% of clients had a financial plan run for them. That amazed me! As I mentioned earlier, our team had run financial plans for every client that would let us from day one in 1995. So, we knew we wanted to offer planning services.

In addition to running financial plans, we also wanted to help clients design their estate plans. We also place this service in our "Strategy" Quadrant. I could write another book on what should be improved within the estate planning industry. Suffice it to say that we believe the problem generally revolves around a lack of deep engagement with families to understand their true desires when passing on more than just their wealth.

This brings me naturally to the Third Quadrant of services we call "Family." We define Family services as getting the first generation on the same page. We do this by listening to the story of their lives and helping them tease out their values.

This process naturally leads us to the Fourth Quadrant we call "Legacy." We define Legacy as the game plan for the second and third generations (and beyond). There is an old saying in our industry that says most families are "shirtsleeves to shirtsleeves" in three generations. However, the research shows that the reason for the money disappearing (and more importantly, the values disappearing) is not poor technical planning, but poor communication. Our goal is to change that.

The third big idea we had in terms of offering Complete Representation was to build a platform for advisors that encouraged collaboration. We believe the business needs to "grow up" and become more professional with specialists doing marketing, relationship management, investments, and service. There are too many "one-man bands" in the industry, and we wanted to deliver better outcomes for clients by creating a "symphony" of collaborating specialists.

As I write this, we are in our third year of operation as an independent firm. The biggest surprise for me has been how much *fun* I am having. Fun is not the first word that I would have expected to use when we launched! It took an immense amount of work, and we are thankful to the clients and team members that have made it so great to come to work every day. I attribute the joy I feel in the business to one thing—total alignment with God's calling.

I felt like we were accomplishing about half of what we wanted to get done while we were at Morgan Stanley. God gave me a vision for how we could get closer to 100%. I trusted Him and left behind all kinds of deferred compensation and perceived safety to pursue that dream. I figured that this new platform would deliver twice the joy the old platform did (50% x 2, right?). The surprise was that the joy He delivered was *exponential*.

As I sit here and write these words, my prayer is that everyone who reads these words will get to that place—a place of total alignment with God's will for their life.

Trading Tip #9

Align your circumstances with your vision. Once you are clear about God's calling on your life, align your circumstances for maximum positive impact. Invite others to join you on your journey!

Question to Ponder

What do you need to do to better align your circumstances and fulfill your calling?

10

Conclusion

The strength and happiness of a man's life consists in finding out which way God is going and going in that direction too.

—Phillips Brooks

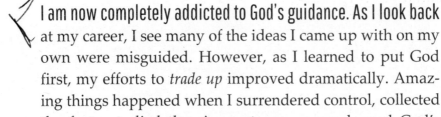 I am now completely addicted to God's guidance. As I look back at my career, I see many of the ideas I came up with on my own were misguided. However, as I learned to put God first, my efforts to *trade up* improved dramatically. Amazing things happened when I surrendered control, collected the facts, studied the circumstances, prayed, read God's Word and sought godly wisdom from like-minded believers. By now, it has become abundantly clear that the secret which enabled me to *trade up* to a more fulfilling life as a financial advisor was simple. The secret was to consistently and dependently look at my business through God's lenses and plug into a power source much bigger than my abilities.

Even after having financial success, I wasn't getting anywhere close to satisfying my desire to have a meaningful career. Though success in business was plentiful, significance in life was still eluding me. Thankfully, God did not leave me in that place. He compelled me to dig deeper into His Word for answers. It was there that He taught me that the path to fulfillment started with a proper relationship with Him. For years, I had written business plans and asked God to bless those plans. I learned that I had it backward. I was treating God as though He was some cosmic vending machine. Reading the Bible made it abundantly clear who was in charge—and it *absolutely* wasn't me. The great bonus in letting God take the lead was that I finally figured out that God wasn't leading from an intention to restrict my fun. Quite the opposite! He wanted to lead so that He could take me to that joy-filled place where I could use all of the experience and talents that He gave me in a way that best glorified Him and most blessed others. I learned that if I would humble myself and ask for His guidance, God would construct a more fulfilling and enjoyable plan for me than I could ever conceive. Here are just a few of the passages He used to powerfully speak to me:

"For I know the thoughts that I think toward you," says the Lord, "thoughts of peace and not of evil, to give you a future and a hope." (Jer. 29:11)

Trust in the Lord with all your heart, and lean
   not on your own understanding;
in all your ways acknowledge Him, and He
   shall direct your paths. (Prov. 3:5-6)

The humble He guides in justice, and the
humble He teaches His way. (Ps. 25:9)

Once I had the head knowledge about who was in charge, I had to say "goodbye" to my old, tired path. That path only led to increasing emptiness. I needed to *trade up*. *Trade up* to a new, vibrant life which would bring a sense of fulfillment and deep-seated satisfaction that had been eluding me. It was time to trade in success and *trade up* for significance.

In the transition, God used all kinds of people to direct me along that path. He used my daughter, Ally, to push me to deeper Bible study. He used a business associate, Pat Combs, to direct me to *Half Time*. He used Bob Buford's coaching in *Half Time* and *Game Plan* to wake me up to the realization that I could have meaning without moving to an African village. He used one of my late father's mentors to teach me that I had to be fully living what I wanted to teach, which forced some much-needed personal change.

He used old acquaintances, like Peter Forbes, to plug me into a whole world of people that was already teaching the lessons I had just learned. Thanks to Peter, I found Ron Blue, an ideal mentor, someone who had already turned his financial services practice into a ministry and had written multiple books on the topic. Peter plugged me into organizations like Kingdom Advisors, National Christian Foundation, Generous Giving, and Crown Ministries that could help me be a more effective steward of my client relationships, helping me to engage in deeper conversations with clients about how to connect their money to their values.

He brought me a mentor in Bob Shank of The Master's Program who challenged me to step it up as a leader and expand our team to fulfill the mission God gave me.

In the last 14 years, God has completely transformed my work life. Although I work in the same industry, I am in a completely new and better place.

He has given me a new level of joy at work because I know that I am now using my gifts to glorify Him and serve others. I am surrounded each day by an amazing group of people who are on the same mission. None of those fun things happened before I gave the business over to God, so He gets *all* the credit!

While God has taken my business to places that I could never have dreamed of on my own, the greatest work He did was in my heart. In His grace, He revolutionized my life. He turned it upside down and inside out. He changed my whole outlook on success and significance. He taught me that everyone who loves God, regardless of the tax status of their employer, is in full-time ministry!

God does not promise us financial success when we turn everything over to Him. It just turns out, in my case, that when you live in a free, capitalist society and try to serve the socks off of people, good things financially can and often do happen. A marketplace book which demonstrates this very well is entitled, *The Go-Giver* by Bob Burg and John David Mann. In it, they write,

> All the great fortunes in the world have been created by men and women who had a greater passion for what they were giving—their product, service or idea—than for what they were getting.

Elsewhere they write,

> Your income is determined by how many people you serve and how well you serve them ... Your compensation is directly proportional to how many lives you touch.

In just a few years, God has taken our team from a four-person group focused on building financial plans and investing the money to a full-blown company that strives to radically love clients and help change the way the world thinks about money.

God has been incredibly gracious to me in allowing me to *trade up* from a plain vanilla career to a thrilling adventure in blessing His people. I invite you to join in the adventure. There are over 600,000 people in the United States alone that are registered to sell securities and a similar number of CPAs. There are also over 1 million lawyers in the U.S., many who practice estate planning.

How would the world look if less than 10% of those folks, say 100k advisors, changed their lives by adopting a lifestyle where they acknowledged that God owns it all? What would it look like if they then let Him direct their business plan and changed the way they taught about money? Once advisors experienced the freedom from the love of money, how many clients would they affect? If each advisor had 100 clients, that would mean a 100x multiplier. This multiplier sounds familiar...

> Then Peter began to say to Him, "See, we have left all and followed You."
>
> So Jesus answered and said, "Assuredly, I say to you, there is no one who has left house or

brothers or sisters or father or mother or wife or children or lands, for My sake and the gospel's, who shall not receive a hundredfold now in this time—houses and brothers and sisters and mothers and children and lands, with persecutions—and in the age to come, eternal life. But many who are first will be last, and the last first." (Mk. 10:28-31)

Based on the hypothetical numbers I laid out, 10 million households would find freedom from the love of money in the U.S. alone. How many marriages would improve from a better perspective on money? How many more people would come to understand that money is just a tool that can help in the cause of loving others, but not a goal in and of itself? Would generosity explode? What problems in the world could be solved by that generosity?

Of course, the greatest problem of the world will continue—the sinfulness and depravity of men's hearts. As Jeremiah put it,

The heart is deceitful above all things, and desperately wicked; who can know it? (Jer. 17:9)

The great news of the Gospel is that it gives us the chance to *trade up* from our old hearts to new ones.

I will give you a new heart and put a new spirit within you; I will take the heart of stone out of your flesh and give you a heart of flesh. (Ez. 36:26)

I *traded up* for that new heart when I was a young boy. I hope you have done the same. Only one thing remained after that—to *trade up* for a new life that was in sync with the new heart God provided. The greatest discovery of my life has been that turning over my life and business to God was the greatest favor I have ever done for myself. I traded success for significance. I traded the lie that full-time ministry is primarily done in non-profits for the truth that *all believers are in full-time ministry everywhere.* Regardless of your profession, I ask you to join me in making those same, eternally profitable trades!

Trading Tip #10

Trade a job for a mission. Understand your unique position in people's lives and the Kingdom influence God may enable you to have.

Question to Ponder

What do you want written as the epitaph on your tombstone in 20 words or less?

Epilogue

Why do you spend money for what is not bread, and your wages for what does not satisfy? Listen carefully to Me, and eat what is good, and let your soul delight itself in abundance.

—Isaiah 55:2

As I look back over my life, one reality dominates and overshadows everything else, and that is the wild, fierce, relentless, stunningly irrational, and utterly unpredictable grace of God. It is this wholly undeserved, magnificent kindness of our Father that has blindsided me time and again. He chased me down when I turned the other way, placed people in my path, orchestrated events, blocked my plans, rerouted my course, and above all else, as the psalmist puts it, "brought" me "out into a wealthy place" (Ps. 66:12). Yes, a wealthy place financially. But most of all, a wealthy place spiritually. And that, my friend, is a wealth nothing on this earth can provide or compare with.

One of my absolute favorite quotes comes from Thomas Carlyle in his book *Sartor Resartus*:

Man's unhappiness, as I construe, comes of his greatness; it is because there is an Infinite in him,

which with all his cunning he cannot quite bury
under the Finite.

Too much of my life has already been spent trying to
fill the God-sized vacuum inside me with earth-sized commodities. And, as Carlyle puts it, with all my cunning, I
could never do it. Tennis couldn't do it. An Armani suit
couldn't do it. Promotions and benefits couldn't do it.
Money certainly couldn't do it. A fantastic job couldn't do
it. And even a great wife and children couldn't do it. Ironically, it was Carlyle's wife who wrote, "I married Carlyle
for ambition; he has far surpassed my wildest expectations,
but I am miserable."

Sheerly by God's grace, I have discovered the way out
of the unhappiness and lack of satisfaction brought inevitably by mere success and prosperity. It's what this whole
book and the greatest discovery of my life is all about. You
have to *trade up*. *Trade up* from success to significance. *Trade
up* from a life that is self-directed to one that is God-teth-
ered. *Trade up* from seeing one's job as a money field to seeing it as a mission field. *Trade up* from enduring life to
attacking it. Most of all, *trade up* our tired, worn out, wanna-
be gods for the true, living God. The only God who never
tires and who alone can fill that God-shaped vacuum He
placed in our souls. The only God who provides a significance to life that cannot be matched by anything this earth
has to offer. The only God who makes good on His promise:

> I, the LORD, am your God, Who brought you up
>   from the land of Egypt;
> Open your mouth wide and I will fill it.
> (Ps. 81:10)

At least that's been my experience. I hope it is yours as well. God bless you, my fellow trader.

Bob Bufano
Lloyd Reeb
Ron Blue   Lupton
NCF

- Disillusionment
- "All In"
- Stewardship is Freeing
- My brao - need giving as antidote